ALMOST

A terrifying true story of an innocent boy
who survived twenty years of abuse.

SHIKESH SORATHIA

Edited by Shikesh Sorathia.
Published by Shikesh Sorathia.

The events described in this book are all true and to the best of
Shikesh Sorathia's knowledge, including the names of people
mentioned.

ISBN-13: 978-1-9164576-0-7

DEDICATION

I am dedicating this book to humanity because we all have a very
important lesson to learn.

EPIGRAPH

"I am not a victim, I am a witness, so it is my duty to give a testimony in order to eventually heal lives and stop abuse."

- Shikesh Sorathia

CONTENTS

AUTHOR'S NOTE

I have left out the names of people involved, including the names of places where the events happened.

By writing this book, I am telling my side of the story.

Throughout my book, you will hear my raw emotion of the traumatic journey that I have been on which I have written as a timeline.

I have written the dialogue in a way which has allowed me to not cause any confusion to what was said and by whom during the events.

I have included a chapter which shows images from my parents diaries, and so on, to highlight the abuse that they almost got away with. By showing the evidence, I hope that it will help the authorities in understanding what needs to be improved so no one else has to suffer the way I did.

I have shared my story for two main reasons. My first reason is to highlight the **WARNING SIGNS** which the authorities didn't notice, and my second reason is to give strength and a voice to those who have experienced similar events as myself, so they can also break away from their past to start a new life and find happiness in their own unique way.

ACKNOWLEDGMENTS

I want to thank every single person who I have met until today because without your love and support, I wouldn't be the man that I am today and this book wouldn't have been possible.

Avril and family,

Keep Smiling and Shining and don't stop being who you are truly meant to be!

God bless,

Shiresh S

Chapter One

The Road To Hell

It all began before my birth and if my parents had signed a paper, then I wouldn't have even taken my first breath on this earth. I wasn't aware of this event until a few years ago when my father told me all about it.

My mother was due for her scan at the hospital and on that same day, both of my parents were being told that their unborn child had down-syndrome which the nurse could see in the scan.

Both of my parents were born in India, so they couldn't understand what they were being told. A nurse tried convincing my parents to sign a paper which would have given the hospital permission to end the pregnancy.

When my father realised what was being asked of him, he became furious because he wasn't just being asked to end the pregnancy; he was also being questioned on how he would look after the son which he already had if he was to give more of his attention to his new son who had down-syndrome?

My father couldn't believe what he was having to hear and in his reply, he told the nurse that he would take his new baby to India and look after him if she felt his new baby would become such a burden.

As my parents didn't give their signature on the form, they received another appointment at another hospital to have a second opinion before deciding on what they would do.

After attending the new appointment, my parents felt relieved to hear that their new baby didn't have down-syndrome.

The nightmare wasn't over for my parents because the big day had then arrived! My mother felt that she was going into labor, so my father drove her to the hospital. They both waited for the nurse before being told that it would still be another two or three days until my mother would give birth.

My mother went home as she didn't want to stay in the hospital. Once my parents reached home, my mother was in the middle of making tea when she had to use the bathroom. She realised that her waters had broken, so my father drove her to the hospital.

As the top of my head was showing, my father drove at a slow speed to make sure that I wasn't born in the car. As soon as my parents got to the hospital, my mother laid down on the bed and with no oxygen or medication, she gave birth.

On Sunday 22nd September 1991 at 9:50pm, I opened my eyes and cried.

At two years of age, I became very unwell and my father believes that his second eldest brother's wife had poisoned me. She wasn't seen for a few days, so my father assumed that she had run away to make it seem like she wasn't to blame. It's not a one hundred percent certainty whether this happened and if it is what happened, then the reason to why it did isn't known.

As I now fast-forward three more years, I was five years of age. My father had a friendship with a guy who he had met through his eldest brother. My father would go over to his place and his friend would come over to ours.

No parent would even imagine that their child would experience sexual abuse by someone who they trusted. My father's friend had a son and he must have been in his mid-late teenage years.

When my father would go over to their place, he would take me and my eldest brother with him. The four separate occasions when it happened at their place, I am uncertain whether my eldest brother had come with us and if he came, then he was playing with the guy's sister in her room.

I was playing with a football in the living room while my father was sitting with his friend talking and drinking beer. As I kicked the football a little too high, it almost knocked the beer over, so my father told me to play with his friend's son in his room.

There were board games laid out on his bedroom floor, so I played with them before he joined in. After a few minutes, he directed me to sit on his bed before putting something in my mouth.

At five years of age, you don't understand what is happening when you're being abused, so when you get older; you realise what you were being told to do which leaves you feeling helpless inside. Even the comments which you're having to listen to during the abuse leaves you questioning what it means?

I wasn't aware of what it all meant? All I knew was that something was wrong. There were moments when I would try to convince him to play the board games a little longer while hoping that my father would knock on the door to say it was time to go.

I cried at one point and when my father asked why, the guy who abused me spoke for me and reassured my father that he did nothing, and didn't know the reason. What would I have even said if I was to speak up? I didn't know what happened, so what words would I have even used to describe it?

Being at school is always fun even though homework can be a pain. When you're sitting at your desk in class after lunchtime, you have a few minutes to talk to your friends about what you did over the weekend.

This wasn't something that I understood because I had realised how different my life was from other children in my class.

"You must love looking through windows," a classmate replied.

I shared what I had done the night before which wasn't something that any of the other children at school were doing. My father was experiencing car crime, so he used to tell me and my eldest brother to take turns in observing his car at night.

We have all seen movies where the children are detectives and have enjoyed investigating something. What I was being told to investigate wasn't any fun at all! There was a notepad and a pen, a phone, a remote to ring the bell downstairs and a pair of binoculars.

My father told me to write every single movement that I saw and if I witnessed his car being damaged, then I would need to call the police before informing him.

Over the past few years, I have spoken to many parents, and they have all told me the same thing of never involving their children in what they may have been experiencing. By knowing this, it makes me realise how much I have missed out on during my childhood.

Have you ever experienced a moment where you felt that you would never see someone again who hurt you in the past, and then it feels like you cannot move when they are right there?

I was seven years of age and playing darts upstairs in the games room. The doorbell rang and by hearing the voices, I could tell that it was my father's friend who had brought his wife, son, and daughter for a quick visit before going to do shopping.

My father's friend's son came upstairs and locked the door. He then had his jeans and pants around his ankles as he directed me to sit between his legs while he laid on the floor face down. I was being directed to have my tongue between his buttocks and to say certain things which he wanted to hear.

Why didn't I shout or scream? Should I have called for my mother? Would crying have saved me? These are the questions which went through my mind after it happened.

I was certain that I would tell my father once they had left. I had built up so much anger to just say it and not frighten away any longer! An argument then took place between my parents and that's when I stayed quiet.

There were moments after this day when my father took me over to their new house which they moved into and the guy who abused me would be there. His presence kept me quiet and frightened as I didn't know what would happen. As my eldest brother was with me, I felt safe by knowing he wouldn't be able to abuse me.

We learn so much in school and one thing which we always hear is how we should respect our parents and always do what they are telling us because they know what is best?

Our parents are people who we think would never hurt us because they will always love and care for us, yet when you hear such hurtful words, it leaves you questioning if they truly love you?

One morning before school, I wasn't feeling well and also knew that my father would go to visit my mother because she wasn't at home. My father forced me to go to school even when I told him I didn't feel well.

When I got to school, my teacher asked me why I was crying and this is where I told her that my father forced me to go to school even when I didn't feel well. The thought of my teacher asking my parents on parents' evening about that day made me feel afraid, so I told my mother, and eldest brother myself after school had finished that same day. Once we got home, my mother told my father all about it.

"You don't deserve to come out with me anywhere or sit in my car anymore," my father said.

Anyone would think that I did something wrong? My father must have known how my teacher would understand his concern of making sure I was in school?

The same evening, I was eating dinner and can still remember what I had on my plate. Fish fingers, hash brown, and potato waffles. While I was eating, my father was standing with my eldest brother while looking at me.

"You are not good enough to be a brother in this family. Your mother is pregnant and we may have a better brother, so we don't need someone who will talk about me to other people. If you want to open the front door and leave, you can," my father said.

I cried. "You wouldn't care if I opened the front door and left?"

"No, I wouldn't. Cry in the passage because we don't want to see you."

While sitting on the stairs and crying, I was looking at the front door and questioning whether I should have opened it and left? I couldn't understand why my father would say such a thing? I wanted to know his answer, so I decided to not leave. Even at seven years of age, I had such strength to go on a mission in wanting to know why my father had said such words? My parents laughed as I cried on the stairs, and I wasn't even allowed to finish my dinner!

We hear about it all the time where so many people grow up and never understand the abuse that they had experienced as a child. So many people grow old without even dealing with the side effects which they have lived with. During a sex education class in year six, we watched a cartoon version which confirmed that what I experienced at the ages of five and seven; it wasn't okay.

I stopped wondering what had happened because now I was aware and knew what it all meant. The question which I now had would take me on a journey in understanding the meaning of two guys performing sexual acts together.

As children, we all hope for magic and fairytales. We watch Disney movies and wish for happiness where we can be superheroes or princesses. After experiencing abuse at such a young age, we hope that we wouldn't have to experience anything more during our childhood. As we get older, we realise that life is unpredictable.

I was walking to school with two girls one morning in year six. There were roadworks going on, on my road, so I had to walk on the road a little before coming back onto the footpath. This is where a car didn't stop and almost ran me over.

The same thing happened the very next day, and it was a lady who lived on my road where her husband admitted in court to damaging my father's car. I told my father about this and he decided to get permission from both girls' parents, so we could report the incident to the police.

You would think that when there are three children who knew what happened, the police would have a strong enough motive to support the crime prosecution service in taking the case to court for a successful trial.

The complete opposite happened where my father told me at the time that the police believed myself, and my two friends were too young to stand trial in court? The lady who tried to run me over told the police that she was inside her house on both days cleaning.

It's never easy for any parent to hear that there is a possibility how their child may not survive. The amount of worrying and questions which any parent would experience would create fear, helplessness, and depression. It would also make any parent wish that they could just click their fingers and everything would be okay. During my childhood, there were several visits to the doctor and hospital because I wasn't able to eat which kept me very weak.

My parents would hear the same thing on every visit how if I didn't eat, then I would die. This made my parents believe that the poison which my auntie may have given to me at two years of age, it had destroyed my body inside which is why I couldn't eat.

Have you ever had a neighbour who has been coldhearted towards you where you have questioned why they would behave in the way that they did? Maybe you're that neighbour who likes to treat others with disrespect?

There was a time in my childhood when my father sat me and my eldest brother down as he explained how he had asked the neighbour living in front of us to move their car from in front of our house, and they didn't do so within the five minutes they said they would.

This is where my father told me and my eldest brother on what to say to them as he was taking us to their house, so they would move their car. My eldest brother didn't say his part which left me saying it instead. What can you even say when you're being told by your own father to swear at someone?

After this incident, my father took my eldest brother and myself out and while he was driving, he questioned why I took time in saying what he told me to say. I explained how my eldest brother didn't say his part which left me confused.

My father then realised this and while looking through his mirror, he looked at me and questioned why I showed fear? What reply could I have even given to such a question? Throughout my childhood, I always wondered if other children had to experience the same things and if not, then why me?

After every negative experience, you hope that nothing else will happen. You wonder when it all would stop, so you can at least not fake a smile anymore while telling everyone "you're okay."

"If you ask me to take you bowling again, then I will throw you in the skip and drive away," my father said.

All I wanted was to go bowling, and it felt like I had done something so wrong? My father would tell me how I was too skinny, so I wouldn't be able to carry the bowling ball.

I don't know which is worse? For my father to tell me that he would throw me in the skip and drive away or for him to tell me that I already looked dead, so if he was to hit me, then I would die?

His phone had gone missing in the house which made him accuse me for not finding it and because he blamed me, he felt that it was okay to say such a thing even after knowing that I could have died for not being able to eat.

It seems like I have always attracted people to seek my guidance which has then given them the answer to what they need to do in order to make the right decision. Even during my late childhood years, a lady approached me who wanted my guidance.

"He is asking me to divorce him and leave... what do you think I should do?" my mother asked.

"I don't think you should leave. Just stay and see what happens."

When you're in your late childhood years and you're being asked to give relationship advice, you don't quite know what to say.

Do you remember when I explained how so many people grow old without even dealing with the side effects from the abuse that they may have experienced as a child?

I broke my silence during my late childhood to my eldest brother. I was lying on my bed while he was sitting on a chair.

"Do you know the guy whose house we go to? He made me suck his dick," I said.

"Why are you telling me... why don't you tell dad?"

I felt fear. "I don't know... I will tell him when the time is right. You don't tell him, I will tell him myself."

After a few days, my eldest brother and myself had the same conversation while we were waiting for our father as we were visiting our grandparents. This was the last time we talked about it and as I remembered my father telling me how I was too young in the eyes of the police from the incident where I almost got run over, I promised myself to tell no one else because who would have believed me?

I wasn't just afraid of my father from the things which he had said. I was also afraid of him because I was witnessing domestic violence between him and my mother.

"Don't hit her! Don't hit her!" I commanded.

There was a time when I couldn't keep quiet because hearing my mother being beaten and not being able to see if she was okay was too painful!

My father explained how everyone was driving him crazy, including his own children? I kept talking back which made my eldest brother tell me to shut up. All I could do was look at my eldest brother and make him realise that I wasn't willing to stay quiet any longer.

Experiencing crime is traumatising, isn't it? What about when you're being made to believe how you experienced something which didn't even happen? It would leave you wondering why someone would want you to believe it?

"When I was coming home from school, two guys stopped me and told me to tell my father to keep his mouth shut or else," I replied to the police officer.

My father brainwashed me with a false incident for two weeks and as I was only a child who had already experienced a lot of abuse, it was easy for him to manipulate me. While sitting in the police station, I wanted to tell the police officer that it was all a lie and then I remembered how my father was beating my mother which kept me silent as I felt very scared.

My father had it all planned out from what happened, where it happened, the ethnic of the guys and even what they were wearing. He wasn't too pleased when I said the colour blue to describe the turban because he felt that Sikh people only wear a black-coloured turban. Was my father afraid of getting caught from my answer to the police officer?

A week after visiting the police station, I received a phone call from a police officer who gave me an option to go to court.

"I don't think there is any point in going to court because there is no CCTV around those houses, so nothing will happen," I replied to the police officer.

Why did my father brainwash me with such a traumatising lie and what was he looking to gain?

"That's the one we made up, didn't we?" my eldest brother said to my father.

"Never say that! I never admit to a lie and you shouldn't either!"

I soon realised that my father had made my eldest brother lie to the police also.

Soon after something would happen, it wouldn't be the end because something else would occur. I accepted that I wouldn't have a normal life for a long time and this made me question my existence?

"If I would suffer for so many years from my birth, then why was I given this life?" I would think to myself.

I was in my early teenage years when my father took me to a nearby road. He parked his car and opened the bonnet.

"What's wrong with his car now?" I thought to myself.

A few minutes had passed and my father was still doing something under the car bonnet, so I got out of the car to see what he was doing. He was holding a knife and a tissue and after he cut through a pipe, he started the engine.

"The pipe is leaking!" I shouted.

My father switched the engine off and cleaned off the pipe and the knife before closing the bonnet. Once we were sat in the car, he handed me the dirty tissue.

"What am I going to do with this?" I thought to myself.

From the strong smell, I realised that my father cut the petrol pipe. Before my father started the car to drive home, I threw the tissue outside of the car as the smell was unbearable. After a short drive we arrived home.

"Throw the tissue in the bin, okay?" my father said.

"I already threw it on the road before we left."

"You should never visit a scene twice once you have committed a crime."

I couldn't understand what he meant? We then went to the same place and picked up the tissue. It wasn't a windy day, so the tissue had remained where I threw it.

My father was furious with me the whole evening once we got home and when I questioned what he did, he told me he did nothing.

"But you cut the pipe, I saw you! You cut the pipe!" I replied.

My eldest brother then joined in and also told me that nothing happened. He wasn't even with us, so how did he know what happened and what didn't?

How can you have someone witness something and then tell them it never happened? This is where I realised that my eldest brother starting believing that it was okay to lie.

Have you ever had one of those moments where you think what you had experienced in the past would never happen again until it does? I was twelve years of age when my eldest brother showed me porn. He was fourteen years of age at the time as he is two years older than me. After showing me porn, he stripped off and abused me.

It happened on four separate occasions in the house and then once in a swimming pool at a health club. Even though he witnessed me choking as I came up from under the water, he had me do the same thing again of having his penis in my mouth.

Both of my parents were away for the weekend to see a psychic whom my father had met. This is the reason why my eldest brother had me all alone for two days when it happened at home. I am uncertain whether my grandmother went with my parents or whether she was downstairs.

Could anyone have witnessed what happened in the swimming pool? There were people swimming under the water and if anyone saw, then I wonder if they ever raised this concern to someone in the health club?

Keeping one secret was already too much to deal with, so having to keep another secret, it haunted me for so many years.

"What if he abuses me again?" I thought to myself.

My eldest brother owned a pellet gun, and I asked him if I could play with it in the garden.

"If you let me hump you, I will," he said.

I assumed that "humping" meant play fighting until he had me face down on the bed with him over me. Our parents were downstairs, so he remained dressed.

"Stop! Get off me! Stop it now!" I commanded.

He said nothing and kept going which made me so angry and even though he let me play with his pellet gun for a quick five minutes; I didn't know how to feel or even what to feel?

He also taught me how to masturbate and as I look back now to when it all happened, I knew too much at a young age which is something that I didn't need to know. By being taught how to masturbate and being shown porn, it became an addiction until nineteen years of age.

Life is hard, it's complicated, and you wonder why you experience so much abuse? You always question why it has to be you? I guess it all depends on what your beliefs are about life and death. Growing up too fast wasn't just about knowing too much, it was also about knowing what it meant to do the right thing.

The school bell rang, and it was time to go home. All of the students rushed out of their classrooms to go home. Everyone was talking, laughing, and some unhappy from not having a nice day.

I waited for my eldest brother beside the trees in the playground as we always walked to school and back home together. On this day, he wasn't there to walk home with me.

"He might be in detention?" I thought to myself.

Ten minutes went by, so I walked around the school to look for him. After an unsuccessful search, I walked home alone.

"Did he forget to pick me up? What if something happened to him and I wasn't told? I thought to myself.

After a short walk, I reached home. I could hear the doorbell ringing inside of the house, yet no one answered the door. I rang the doorbell again and there was still no answer.

"What should I do? I could go for a walk and then come back?" I thought to myself.

While looking around, I saw my eldest brother walking towards the house with his friend laughing at God knows what.

"Where were you?" I asked.

He didn't give a full reply and I could see that he was panicking because he knew our father would hit him. He has witnessed domestic violence also and has received beatings himself by our father, so it's understandable that he was going out of his mind.

I knew that the right thing was to tell our parents, and this is where my eldest brother panicked even more while he begged me not to tell them.

"If you tell them, I will kill myself," he said.

My mind went blank, I felt so helpless and didn't know what to do because while he said those words; he was holding a knife to this throat.

Something kept telling me to still tell our parents. It wasn't a surprise to witness my parents so furious when they got home. My father slapped my eldest brother across the face and the look which my eldest brother gave me didn't bother me because I had now built strength in knowing what it meant to do the right thing and that was to never stay quiet!

At the end of every year, I always reflect on what I have learnt, what I will leave behind, and what I will take into the New Year.

At the start of every New Year, I go through another reflection which allows me to understand what I could do that year which would bring me closer to my dreams. I also reflect on what sort of person I wish to become and who I wish not to be. Sometimes, I didn't want to care about who I may have become to keep myself safe.

It was a Sunday morning where my father would take me and my eldest brother to a place where the Hindu community would gather for worship. On our way there, my father was testing me to see if I had studied my times tables. I wasn't interested in learning about times tables because I was still processing the sexual abuse which I had experienced by two different guys.

We arrived at the place, and my father parked his car. I was sitting in the front passenger seat touching my lip with my finger and checking if it was still bleeding. My lip had swelled up, and I had to tell everyone who asked that I had experienced an allergic reaction that morning.

What would have people thought or even done if I had told them that my father had hit me on my mouth with his fist while we were on our way because I got a few questions wrong about Maths?

My father began telling me, and my eldest brother about what both my parents and grandparents had experienced by their families. The names and addresses was something which I had to remember because my father also explained how if he was murdered, then I knew where "my enemies" lived?

My father would say something like, "You and your brothers will not be safe if I don't stop them. Your mother's family, my family, neighbours, doctors, hospital, police, social services, politicians and schools are all part of a paedophile ring. They want to take you and your brothers for witchcraft."

It was all too confusing, and I was only thirteen years of age. After a few weeks, my eldest brother and myself went to a nearby park with our father where he taught us how to break glass bottles to cause physical harm if we ever needed to defend ourselves.

The way my father was telling me everything, and the "self-defense training" which he was having me experience, seemed like I was being trained to hunt people and kill them.

My father would also say something like, "If I don't harm the paedophile ring and stop them, your wife and kids will not be safe when you get married, so I have to do this."

It wasn't too long until he made me believe how I would also need to harm the paedophile ring and go to prison to prove that I wasn't a coward?

"If I have to go to prison for harming the paedophile ring, then what is the point of getting married and having children?" I would think to myself.

There were also at least two occasions where my eldest brother and myself witnessed our father pouring brake fluid over someone's car. He told my eldest brother to do the same thing on two occasions. It seemed like crime was the main motive for my father?

My father had also drilled a small hole under the door handles of his car, and he had purchased a long metal rod which he had sharpened on one end if not both.

Every time we would come back home, my father would tell my eldest brother to put the rod through the hole and for me to hold it on the other end to help him while our father would drive at a slow speed. This would cause a long scratch on the side of a car. The owner of the car was the neighbour who my father had convicted in court for damaging his car. My father would say something like, "An eye for an eye."

Have you ever felt unheard? Where your concerns about something serious wasn't important to someone?

"Give me the phone, and I will phone him then!" I commanded my mother.

We were on our way to do shopping when something fell at the back of the car. It kept making a loud noise, so my mother parked the car on the side of the road. We both checked the back of the car and saw a big round metal plate hanging off from under the car. I told her to call my father more than once, and she refused.

Instead of listening to me, she unhooked the metal round plate, and put it in the boot of the car before driving home. The only time she told my father about it was when we got home.

My father went with my eldest brother and realised what had happened. Once they sorted everything out, they came back home. My father explained how the metal plate was holding the spare tire in place, and because the bolt became loose, it had fallen.

My parents argued, and my father also realised that my mother didn't listen when I told her to phone him.

It's understandable that my mother feared of getting into trouble however, not listening to her own son in such a serious situation is neglect in my eyes. If something has happened to your car, then you would want to make sure that it's safe to drive again, wouldn't you?

I went to India with my family in 2006 when I was fourteen years of age, and we visited someone in the name of "Holy Man." His place was a five-hour drive, and I didn't understand why we were visiting him. My father soon explained how he had visited him when he went to India at the end of 2002.

My father has told me that he had so much body pain, and even after every medical test was carried out, he still had a lot of pain? The Holy Man told my father that he was a victim of witchcraft, and that was the reason for his pain.

The Holy Man wanted to see my mother because he told my father that she too was a victim of witchcraft, so this was the reason for the visit. We went to his house at least three times before he came to ours to carry out a ceremony to remove the witchcraft.

My mother had to stitch up a black doll, and during the ceremony, we were all asked to cut our nails from both hands and feet, to cut some of our hair, and give a pair of our clothing to complete the ceremony.

After the ceremony, my father told the Holy Man how I wanted to see the spirit which gave him the answers to help people. This is where he said words with a red cloth over his left shoulder and a few minutes later, he started moving his hands back and forth at a fast speed while making a hissing noise of a snake.

My father told me that the spirit which gave him the answers to help people was a spirit of a snake. The Holy Man then opened his eyes real wide, and a loud roar came out of his mouth as he spread his arms wide open.

During that moment, the Holy Man told my father that his eldest son has a "trishul — shorthanded weapon" in the palm of his hand where they could also do the same work as the Holy Man to help people. It seemed like I had just entered a real-life horror movie where I didn't know whether to run or just sit there?

It was now time to come back to the UK, and when we boarded the train, the Holy Man was there to see us away. After the ceremony had ended, he gave us a coconut, and told us that it had a good spirit inside to keep us safe, so we should always pray to it. He also told my parents to carry out some cleansing ceremonies when we reached our house in the UK.

After praying to the coconut a few times, I didn't want to anymore. Once we were back in the UK, the Holy Man phoned my father a few times and explained how a few people needed his help and would pay him at least one hundred thousand pounds each.

This made my father question whether he had found his calling in life and then believed that he was being asked to do witchcraft on people, so he stopped listening to the Holy Man further.

My father also believed how the whole ceremony was a cover up to do another kind of ceremony to control the whole family. He told me how they could make a witchcraft doll with everything that they took such as our clothes. This is where he put the coconut into the river and removed everything from the house which he believed held an evil spirit inside.

It was now time to meet my father's eldest brother. In 2007, my father's eldest brother, his wife, and my father's second eldest brother's daughter came to our house. There was a knock on the window, and then the doorbell rang. As my father had CCTV in front of the house, he saw who it was.

As soon as he opened the door, he slapped his sister-in-law across the face, and in Gujarati, he told her that he kept his promise of slapping her if she ever came to his house. My father's eldest brother then came to the door, and an argument broke out.

I witnessed my father pick up an umbrella, and hit his eldest brother on his head, and on his back. My father's niece tried to stop him by trying to grab a hold of the umbrella. She wasn't able to take the umbrella off my father because he hit her arm with it to stop her.

My father always told me how we needed to stick together if anyone ever came to our house who was "our enemy" and if it led to a fight, then the whole family would have to join in. The way my father always spoke, I didn't want to know what would happen if I went against him, so I swore at his family.

My father's eldest brother looked at my father and said something like, "Watch what I will do to you now!"

My father, my eldest brother and myself followed him because my father's car alarm went off. As we saw my father's niece recording what was happening on her phone, we walked back into the house. I am uncertain whether my mother was at the door, or whether she was still inside. All I know is that my father's family did not step foot in our house that day.

"We only came here to tell you your brother died, and you started a fight!" my father's sister-in-law said in Gujarati.

They then left and came back with the police a few days later to make sure that my grandmother had received the news about her son.

Six months later, police officers came to our house and arrested my father because his family filed a report against him for hurting them. As there wasn't enough evidence for the case to go to court, my father wasn't charged.

It's not nice being blamed for something that wasn't your fault, is it? Where you have broken down in tears while thinking what's the point in even living? This is how I felt in 2009 when my parents blamed me for something that they told me to do.

We arrived home and the neighbour's car was blocking our driveway. My father told me to knock on their door and ask them to move their car. There was no answer for a few seconds until a lady came to the window.

She gave me hand signals and wouldn't come to the door to talk. I didn't know what she was saying, and every time I directed her to the door, she would carry on giving me hand signals.

After a minute, she came out of the house, and moved her car forward. While my father parked his car in front of his driveway, he hit the back of her car. An argument broke out where a man from the same house tried to pull my father out of his car before grabbing my arm and looking towards a white van while saying something like, "Come with me now."

The police then arrived, and they told me that I was to blame and if my father wanted to pursue the case further, then I would be arrested for trespassing?

"If you came to my house, I would grab your arm too!" the police officer said.

I explained to the police officer what happened and instead of listening to what I was saying, he made me feel intimidated. The same evening, and for many more days, my parents blamed me even when I explained that I did nothing wrong as I only did what they told me to do. They didn't accept the part they played and made me feel responsible.

How can you make your own parents understand what happened if they are not willing to accept the truth? My father told me that he hit the neighbour's car because he wanted to which is why the argument occurred. Anytime I have experienced confrontations with the neighbours, it has been because of my father.

It's such a great feeling when you've done something productive where you feel so proud of what you have accomplished, isn't it? Do you remember that time when you achieved something, and couldn't wait to tell someone?

"Dad, I cut the grass today!" I said.

He slapped me across the head. "I told you I would get you if you went against me. The inside of the house needs more cleaning, so why can't you do that first, and then the outside?"

He wouldn't stop telling me to cut the grass, and the time I did what he had asked, I received abuse? I realised that no matter what I did, it was never good enough. If I did what he asked, then I would get abuse, and if I did nothing at all, I would still get abuse?

Turning sixteen should be a beautiful time yet when you realise that you're not appreciated, and supported for what you want to do in your life, you realise that your sixteenth birthday isn't so sweet.

It was the day before my sixteenth birthday when I went downstairs to have a shower.

"Hello, son. So, you're sixteen tomorrow? Do you know what you want to do yet?" my father asked.

"I want to become a DJ, and my own music producer."

"No, that's not right for you. Concentrate on your English, Maths and Science."

If my father even cared about my happiness a little, then he would have asked why I wanted to become a musician. It was because when I was around music, I didn't feel abused. I guess things happen for a reason though, right? The abuse that I had experienced wasn't known to my parents, and if I am honest, I wasn't in a place to be myself because I never had the chance to know what that meant for a long time.

I was now in my final year of high school and my father told me that he didn't want me to fail my GCSE's, so he took my grandmother to India in case she passed away during my exams. She had a lot of health problems and had been in and out of hospital several times over the years.

My eldest brother and myself remained at home in the UK as I needed to get my exam results before enrolling for further education. During the time my eldest brother and myself were all alone, it felt like I was the elder one because I cooked for him, cleaned up after him and kept the house tidy. I also painted the kitchen as my father had told me to do so.

As so many other things had happened, I didn't focus on the abuse that my eldest brother had made me experience, so it didn't affect me as much as I thought it would. When you have experienced so much abuse since your childhood, you learn to cope with everything to keep going and that's exactly what I was doing.

Over the years, my father has told me many theories. He has explained how most of them have come from seeing a psychic from 2003 until 2009. I am uncertain of the exact sum that my father has paid the psychic.

He has told me that he re-mortgaged his house because he had no other way to pay for her services. My whole family has met the psychic because we made countless trips with our father to see her. It was a tiring experience and one which seemed like a waste of time.

My father believed that he found the psychic himself and after growing a belief in witchcraft, he explained that he went because someone possessed him to go as the "paedophile ring" wanted to know what my father knew about them.

There has also been one or two occasions when my father didn't allow me to go to school because he took me to see the psychic. My presence wasn't needed, so to take me out of school is neglect in my eyes. I have remained in the car most of the time because my father wanted to make sure that no one damaged his car.

My father told me that the Holy Man told him to find someone in the UK because he couldn't help him from a distance. The belief of my father being possessed to go to the psychic isn't very accurate because if the Holy Man told him to find someone in the UK and this is what he did, then there can't be another reason.

On the very first visit to the psychic, me and my eldest brother waited in a public place while our father was with her and he didn't tell us where he was going. From the things that the psychic told my father, his trust towards her became a bond because they were all true. This is what my father has told me.

It seems like the amount of trust that my father had towards the psychic, he felt she would solve his problems such as body pains. I couldn't understand most of the things that I was being told.

My father told me something like, "She said, you can say a few words through witchcraft from your house to drain oil out of someone's car and it happens."

There have been some cleansing ceremonies which my father has carried out on all of the family in the house. If anyone had a stomach ache, my father would believe that it was because of witchcraft, so he would have my grandmother hold salt in her hand while saying words. The salt would then be scattered in the middle of the road where three roads would join.

Another ceremony involved sticking cow dung on the wall and hanging a thin rope off it once it had been moved around someone's head seven times. The rope would then be set on fire until it slipped off into a silver dish filled with water.

It was now August 2008, and I got my GCSE results. From all of the distractions, and abuse which I had experienced, I was still a little surprised to find out that I had failed.

My father wanted me to get my exam papers remarked, so this is what I did and the results came back the same. I retook English and Maths with BTEC First in Business and Drama while in sixth form.

I had now turned seventeen years of age and was unaware that what I was told in the past would be a test from my father.

He said something like, "To beat this gang, you have to form your own gang and go after them. If you can, hang around with some guys in school who are a little rough and do whatever they say to prove your loyalty."

My future prospects were looking so bright! I assumed that he was only sharing his thoughts, and when I asked him if he was joking or being serious, he confirmed that he wanted me to form a gang who would support me in whatever I may have done.

I should have quit school that day and should have planned for my funeral because an early death would have been the outcome. It became a daily conversation where my father would tell me to form a gang while also telling me to focus on my education? It seemed like he was telling me to live two different lives?

When you have experienced abuse since your childhood, it becomes very difficult for you not to see the bigger picture in front of your eyes. I believed that I wasn't safe, and if I was to have a wife, and my own children, then they would be in danger which is why I listened to my father because I believed it was the truth. Even though I kept growing older, I still felt like that five-year-old innocent boy who lost himself at a young age.

At the end of the school year on my last day, an incident took place where a few guys within my year including myself, we bricked a guy's house due to racism. We had reported him to his teacher and to the head teacher as the racial remarks didn't stop.

I could have done nothing, and just walked away yet all I could think about was my future and what I would miss out on if I didn't do what my father had told me to do. Neither of us got charged because once the police realised that it happened due to racism, they stepped away.

Once I got home, I assumed that my father would have been proud of me because I had done what he had asked. This wasn't the case because he denied ever telling me to form a gang. I received nothing but physical and verbal abuse that evening, and the verbal abuse carried on for a few weeks.

He said something like, "I thought you would look after your two younger brothers once I was gone, but I was wrong."

I now realised that my father would deny everything and make it look like I was the problem. I couldn't understand why?

My father began sharing his hate for the Sikh and Islamic religion because they have caused him and so many Hindu people a lot of harm in the past.

"It happened so many years ago and just because it was a certain religion, it doesn't mean that every single person within that religion holds the same views," I thought to myself.

I couldn't believe what my father was telling me to do! He told me how I should urinate on a picture of both Sikh and Islamic religion with the media present and declare a religious war with them? He was even telling me to buy a sword and keep it ready for war?

I felt sick to my stomach and I couldn't eat for a few days because of what I had heard. I already knew that my father would deny everything that he had said, so I decided not to mention it.

The same conversation took place a few days later, and I made it clear to my father that I would never do such a thing because I was against it and if it was something which he wished to do, then he would have to do it himself without involving me in his evil plans.

To sit in the same room with my father when he had treated me in such abusive ways and carried such evil views was difficult enough, yet when you have to sleep in the same room, it feels like you cannot breathe!

The only time I could breathe was when he would be out of the house or when I would be at school. Even at school, it would still be torture because at home I would have trouble and in school I would get bullied, so it felt like running from one prison to another.

Can you imagine how suffocated I felt at home by having so much fear within me from my father? Even when I would try to fall asleep, his snoring would still scare me!

When someone has abused you for so many years, everything about them will affect you. Even when they're not in the same room, just hearing their voice will make you panic!

How many of you have made a promise to yourselves and you believed that you would keep it which wasn't the outcome?

My father was arguing with me and like always, it involved emotional and verbal abuse. I felt lost and alone, so I told my father that I would leave home because if he felt that it was okay to treat me in such abusive ways, then it would have been better if I had left.

He always told me that I had an attitude problem and it frustrated me a lot because he didn't understand how hard he made life for me, so I thought it was best to tell him why.

"Before I go, let me tell you why I have always been so angry because you seem to think I have an attitude problem? Do you know that boy whose house we used to go to? He sexually abused me... he made me suck his dick!" I said.

It felt like a horror movie where everything would be silent and then something would make you jump! This is how I felt and deep down, I told myself that I broke my promise and didn't have to keep it any longer. It felt reassuring when my father told me that he believed me which also made me question myself on how I would have reacted if he told me that he didn't believe me?

There was a time during the investigation when my father was telling my eldest brother to lie to the police even if he didn't remember me telling him about the abuse when we were younger. This shocked me, and I couldn't stay quiet!

"There will be no lies in this investigation! If you remember, then you tell them that you remember and if you don't remember, then you tell them that you don't remember!" I commanded

My father looked at me in a way which made me feel like he got frightened from my response. He agreed with me with little confidence showing as I reassured him how it's always best to tell the truth no matter what the outcome would be. I hoped so much that both my father and eldest brother had got my message of not lying to the police because I was the one who experienced the abuse.

It was after that day when I heard both my father and eldest brother arguing downstairs.

"What if he is telling him to lie again?" I thought to myself.

This wasn't my only worry as I still knew that my parents didn't know about their eldest son and what he had done. I didn't understand how I would tell them and when?

My father was convincing me not to report the abuse which I experienced by the family friend because nothing would happen and even though I knew this, I felt that I still had to talk in case he was abusing someone else. I couldn't live with the fact that someone else could experience the same thing and I was just staying quiet?

"Because you reported it to the police, you took the chance away from me and your eldest brother to hurt him," my father said.

"Shikesh! What are you doing? You can't send him to prison!" my father said.

It was one afternoon when I walked downstairs to tell my parents that I needed to speak with them. Fear was all I felt because even though I gained the courage to tell my parents about their eldest son, I didn't know how my father would react. Before I told my parents, I phoned the police officer who was dealing with the case which was already reported and as she was at the scene of a crime, she wasn't able to speak.

My father told me to give another reason for my call and the reason was to mention how my eldest brother had experienced abuse even though he told my father that he wasn't abused.

There was a time when we were both young and had gone to someone's house. The son in that family had called my eldest brother into his room and locked the door without allowing me or his sister into the room. My eldest brother has said nothing happened, so it will remain a mystery.

The way my father looked at me and the way he raised his voice, it scared me. It's understandable that my parents wanted to protect their son, yet when you have heard your own father tell you for so many years how he would never support any form of abuse even if it were his own kids who had done the crime, it leaves you questioning why he would change his perspective?

Maybe he wasn't just saying it anymore, and the time had now come to put his words into action which remained words only.

My father would say something like, "We don't want to be responsible for his death... what do you want me to do, kill him?"

I wasn't staying quiet about the abuse which my eldest brother had made me experience and when my father realised that I was serious about reporting it to the police, he made me believe how if my eldest brother killed himself in prison, the blame would be on me.

Even though what my father was saying scared me, I still wasn't staying quiet because once my silence was broken, I found my voice which allowed me to fight for my innocence.

The reason why my father was trying so hard to keep me quiet is because he asked my eldest brother about the abuse and he admitted to everything in front of me!

When my father ran out of ways to keep me quiet, he used guilt as his last option.

He said something like, "Your grandmother is a witch and she knows how to cast spells. She was taken to Africa at a young age and taught how to possess people. What your brother did to you was because of witchcraft, so don't blame him because it's not his fault."

I became silent after hearing these words because I couldn't handle blaming my eldest brother if it wasn't his fault. When my father realised that I had become silent, his control over me escalated.

Experiencing a robbery in your own house is never nice, is it? What about experiencing a robbery which you didn't even know about? My father found himself in financial difficulties and I had convinced him to sell the gold jewellery which he had as he kept thinking about selling it himself. No one was wearing it, so it seemed like the right choice to make which would have brought my father out of the financial difficulties that he was experiencing.

With no sign of a break in and nothing showing on CCTV, who took the jewellery? My father believes that the "paedophile ring" had a copy of our house key and while we were out, they came in from the back door, used a device to open the safe and took the jewellery without leaving a trace. As there wasn't any CCTV which recorded the back of the house, it remains a mystery or does it?

It was one evening when I heard wardrobes opening and closing in the room that my eldest brother was sleeping in.

"What is he doing?" I thought to myself.

The following morning, I was sitting downstairs with my eldest brother while he waited for our father as he was getting a lift to go to university. His left jeans pocket had a plastic bag with something inside.

"Why is your pocket so full... what's in there?" I asked.

His response wasn't believable, so I asked him again once our father was telling him that he was ready to leave. His response was the same and to even think that he would do such a thing made me feel sick. There was a time when he hid two iPods and then sold them for money. By remembering this incident, it wasn't wrong for me to suspect him.

My eldest brother felt it was okay to lie since his early teenage years, so he didn't confess to taking the iPods until we showed him the receipt of sale which we found in his wardrobe. My father believed that someone was trying to frame him for something which he wouldn't have done, so this is why we searched his wardrobe to see what he may have had that may have got him into trouble.

It was a few weeks after we realised the jewellery was missing when my father received a letter addressed to my eldest brother from a pawnbroker. It didn't state every item, and this is where I told my father that if it's going to be sold in small quantities, then it wouldn't be the only letter which he would receive and I was right!

My eldest brother denied taking the jewellery even though the receipts showed his signature. My father wanted us to check if the jewellery was ours, so after a visit to the pawnbrokers, we knew it was ours with a ring included that we didn't own? I wonder why my father didn't come with us to see the jewellery himself?

My father asked us to make the contract longer because he told us that he was trying to form an investigation. During that time, my eldest brother was experiencing identify fraud which was being investigated by the bank and the police. Once the investigation was over, my eldest brother was in the clear.

After a few months, my father reported the jewellery incident to the police with my eldest brother and as his signature was on the receipts with no evidence to prove another theory, my eldest brother would have been to blame if my father pursued the case further.

We are all aware that life is about giving and when you see someone struggling, you would do anything to help them, wouldn't you? This is what I did where I offered to give my parents one hundred pounds of my EMA bonus which would help them pay the bills.

My father was refusing to take it at first and I told him that I was giving it to him, so he wouldn't need to pay me back. EMA stands for education maintenance allowance which was a scheme available to students aged between sixteen to eighteen for being in full-time education.

I was getting thirty pounds a week and one hundred pounds bonus every Easter and Christmas as long as my attendance was above a certain percentage which it always was. My father convinced me that he would pay me back because he couldn't take money from his own son.

Who would have thought that a kind gesture of helping your parents would be the start of a very painful nightmare? There was even a time when I counted every change coin with my father which we had saved. After counting the coins, the total amount was two hundred pounds. My father told me that it was my money, so it would go into my bank account.

"You know there's a change machine in the supermarket where you could get money there?" the cashier at the bank said.

"Oh, I didn't know that. It's easy to bring the money here though because it's going straight into my bank account," I replied.

The money didn't stay in my account because my father told me to send the money into his account while telling me that he would pay me back.

He also said something like, "The paedophile ring has members working in the bank, so this is why I told you to put the money into your account, and then put into mine because the gang wouldn't know I didn't have money."

"If the paedophile ring has members working in the bank, then they could check his bank account to see how much money he has?" I thought to myself.

My father never gave me a straight answer because there was always a lie involved. He would only explain his actions once he had got what he wanted because he had no other reason to keep making me believe his lie.

"If I will stay hungry after eating a little, then I won't eat at all," I thought to myself.

There were times in college when I didn't eat because my father would take almost all of my money. I needed to keep calm with how much chaos was around me, so I wrote poetry which allowed me to express myself. There was a poetry competition online, so I entered a poem for two different categories.

A few days after the closing date of the competition, I received a letter which informed me that one of my poems came second! The letter also stated that my poem would be in their book and all I had to do was sign a paper and pay for the book.

"What's the point?" I thought to myself.

I had no money because my father took it from me which made me so angry because I could have achieved a lot but instead, I became severely depressed.

I had now turned eighteen years of age and my father was preparing me to go to prison. I was sitting opposite him one evening while crying.

"I am so skinny! Why do you want me to go to prison where there are murderers, rapists and so many others who will hurt me?" I asked.

He looked unconcerned. "You will be okay."

I was taught how to commit a crime and make it look like self-defense. My father believed that I needed to break the paedophile ring by going after them and as long as I claimed self-defense, I would have been okay?

It seems like my father believes that if two adults sleep together outside of their marriage and have a child together, then they are paedophiles?

He would say something like, "This paedophile ring is using a Hindu festival to call each other brother and sister in front of others when behind the scene, they are sleeping around and giving each other kids."

My father also told me that his eldest brother played a part in their father's murder because they didn't get on well?

"Why would your eldest brother do such a thing?" I asked.

"His wife is a witch, so she possessed him and turned him against him. That's why he killed him."

2010 wasn't going well because it felt like each week would break me more than it did in the previous week. It hurt so much when my father made me believe that I would become a paedophile? He told me that it was a fact because people on the news were saying so?

"It's a complete lie!" I commanded.

He gave me an evil look. "It's true, so believe it!"

"How do I stop myself from doing such a thing then?"

"You can't stop it from happening if it will happen."

For three weeks, I tried to come up with a solution to stop myself from ever doing such a thing. Leaving college was also on my mind because I didn't want to be around people after what my father made me believe.

"If I cross that road, then I will deal with it," I thought to myself after thinking about suicide.

Moving out and getting a place of my own was always on my mind. My parents were aware about my intentions and from the emotional abuse which I received from my father, I wasn't able to save up any money because he always took it from me. This was the time when I thought about becoming a male prostitute.

I would think, "All I know is abuse, so it doesn't bother me if I will sell my body. I will have money and will then move out."

Even though I always handed in my homework on time and was never late to school or missed a day unless something had happened, I wasn't prepared to stack shelves because it made me feel like a failure by knowing that I didn't even have the energy to stack shelves? All I could imagine was selling my body because I believed that I was worth that little.

While I was experiencing all of these different thoughts, my father thought that it was best to make me feel more helpless by making me also believe how if I told any girl about my past, then they would see me as damaged goods and wouldn't want to be with me.

"I will just be with someone who has experienced abuse also because that way, she won't be able to see me as damaged goods," I kept thinking.

It was now time to find out what the outcome was for the abuse case which I reported about the family friend.

"Hello, Shikesh?" the police officer asked.

"Yes?"

"I'm just calling about the case... I'm afraid it's bad news."

Even though I was aware how not much could happen, I still felt angry because it's never a nice feeling to know that the person who hurt you got away with it.

A few days later, my father approached me.

"You can look up a solicitor who deals with abuse cases and try for a civil trial," he said.

I wasn't aware about the law and how it worked, so I didn't know what options I had. My father has always known about the law, so I assumed that he was certain and there would be an outcome.

After looking up a few solicitors, I wrote their details and called them while I was in college.

Once I completed my year at sixth form, I didn't want to retake the year again because I still failed my English and Maths exams. It wasn't all bad because I did really good in BTEC First in Business and Drama.

I couldn't bear the thought of failing again, so I studied Motor Vehicle in college and as I had an interest in cars, I knew that I would enjoy it. What I didn't realise is that I would still have to do English and Maths! When you think that you have gotten away with doing something, you bump right into it!

After phoning most of the solicitors, I felt lost because they all offered compensation and it's what I didn't want. There was one solicitor left and after speaking for a few minutes, I said yes because even though they didn't promise an outcome, compensation wasn't the main agenda.

A few days after getting in touch with the solicitor, a lady came to the house to get information from me. Before she left, I had to sign the relevant papers and assumed that it was to start the court process. My father was sitting in the same room as I was signing the papers. To have even the smallest of hope meant so much because I didn't feel worthless.

"Great... It's now the waiting game again!" I thought to myself.

From hearing my father talk about the "paedophile ring" for so many years, it seemed like he would finally hurt someone where I could then live my life with no fears. It was Friday 5th November 2010 when my father approached me in the evening and told me what he was planning to do.

"I will stay drunk tonight and I will then kill someone," he said.

"You can't even stand because you're so drunk. If someone attacks you first, then you will just fall."

I went to sleep that night while thinking, "If my life is in such danger, then why don't I do something myself?"

My second year of college had now begun, and I was still studying Motor Vehicle. I had never worked on cars outside of college and it felt like I was a natural. I had always known that I was good with my hands, so I always preferred the practical side more than the theory. The first time when I changed a tire using the tire machine, my performance was flawless!

"He's already a pro!" a classmate said.

I started believing that there was a reason for me to live and how I wasn't a failure. The fast and furious movies allowed me to dream and my future looked so exciting! When I look back now, it seems like it was just a fantasy which kept me going. That's what it's about sometimes, right? To have a fantasy which keeps you going until you realise what your WHY really is.

During the final months of my second year in college, I couldn't stop thinking about being a DJ because that dream never disappeared. If I started to DJ in that moment, then it would have changed everything for the better!

I was already putting samples together, and I knew that it would have worked! There were a few people with whom I was speaking to online and after receiving positive comments, I felt so uplifted! If I kept practicing and joined a music programme to help me further, then my whole life would have changed forever!

Thunder then struck and when it rained, it poured! I received a letter which stated the compensation I would be receiving. My heart fell because there would be no court case. I still felt so happy because within a few months, I would have finished college and wouldn't need to ask anyone for money.

"Do you think you are worth that much? You should have got fifty thousand pounds," my father said.

It wasn't too long until I realised that my father had debts of fifty thousand pounds and that's why he believed that I should have got that amount.

What made the situation even more unbearable is how I was feeling because my emotional and mental health had suffered throughout college. There was a time during college when I heard voices of people calling my name and after asking my classmates if they had called me, I became aware of how seriously I needed to take the situation.

My father approached me one afternoon when I got home from college and he wanted to talk about something.

"When you were signing the papers, I saw the big writing and knew it was compensation. I didn't tell you because I didn't want to make you feel down," he said.

I thought, "If you cared about me, then you would have stopped me from signing the papers and made me realise what I was signing for!"

A few days later, both of my parents sat down with me.

"Me and your mum have already decided that we won't touch a penny of the compensation. We are making you a God promise, so we won't touch it because of where it's coming from. It's all yours and you have nothing to worry about," my father said.

I checked my bank account on Friday 6th May 2011 and noticed the compensation in my account. I told my father about it that moment and was hoping that he would keep his promise of not touching a penny.

He held out his bank card while looking down. "Give me two."

"Should I send him two pounds instead?" I thought to myself.

When you have experienced financial abuse for so long, you learn the terminology that someone uses to take money from you and this is how I knew that he wanted two thousand pounds.

I felt caged in like my world was taking another dark turn. So many questions were going through my mind and I thought what more could happen?

Within a few months, the compensation was all gone! I received sixteen thousand, five hundred pounds in total. After paying the firm their fee, I had eleven thousand, five hundred and fifty pounds in my account. There was only a small amount which I spent on myself to buy music equipment because I wanted to focus on my DJ career.

Both of my parents and eldest brother benefited with the rest of my compensation. I was being made to withdraw money from my account like I was so rich!

"Why am I experiencing this… why me?" I thought to myself.

There was a moment during the financial abuse where I looked at myself in the mirror and thought, "He isn't going to stop until every penny is gone!"

This brought me peace because I knew that it would keep happening, so it allowed me to prepare myself emotionally and mentally for the next time.

During the financial abuse, my father played with my emotions, hurt me physically, degraded me with words and made me believe how everything would be my fault if I didn't give him the money. He used both of my younger brothers against me and made me feel guilty for situations which would not happen.

The times when I had control over the situation, my father would talk in a sweet voice to make me believe that he meant no harm and once he had control over the situation again, I would have to listen to such verbal abuse which no one should ever have to listen to! He made me feel like a resource and nothing more.

I became aware of what I was experiencing because my curiosity got the best of me. I wanted to know how other people had survived abuse and how they could start a new life. This led me to researching about it online where I came across people sharing their stories.

"If they can do it, then so can I!" I thought to myself.

I learnt about different types of abuse and there were so many lightbulb moments which I experienced while understanding what each type of abuse involved. This allowed me to reflect on what had happened and what was still happening in my life.

It seemed like everything was happening for a reason because the time I became depressed, I learnt that alcohol and drugs would only make my situation worse, so I stayed away from them both.

The way my father harassed me, it made it hard not to think of dying. He would stare at me while I would be eating because he didn't enjoy my complaining of what he was making me experience.

I kept thinking, "Does my father know how to support an abuse survivor?"

My father has supported survivors of many crimes including sexual abuse, so it's not that he doesn't know how sensitive the situation would be. By understanding this, I kept thinking, "Why would he treat me differently then?"

It was now July 2011, and I completed my second year of college. I not only passed Motor Vehicle Level One and Two, I also passed Adult English and Maths!

It felt like I had now completed my education because I didn't need to go to university. The whole education journey wasn't smooth sailing because in every school and college, I got bullied and discriminated by certain students for being born a Hindu.

It wasn't a bad experience just because of bullying and racism; it was also because of what I was experiencing at home. Once I completed my final year at college, I knew that I needed to rest because I was severely depressed, suicidal and my hygiene was the last thing that I thought about.

I don't understand how I passed college because there were so many sleepless nights. As things kept getting worse, I questioned my beliefs because I couldn't understand how I would suffer so much if I had done no wrong?

Even though I was speaking to my college welfare officer, I still felt so alone because I knew no one who was experiencing similar things as I was. There were times when I wanted to run away from home and then didn't because I had no money.

I felt free once I had no money because my father couldn't abuse me for it. This was the case until September 2011 because my father told me to sign onto Job Seeker's Allowance. He gave me different excuses for why I had to and they all made little sense.

My father knew of my situation and how I wasn't fit to work. This didn't stop him from harassing me for two weeks and forcing me to sign onto Job Seeker's Allowance. I had told my father to get me a psychiatrist because I thought about ending my life every day.

He would say something like, "If you tell anyone you want to kill yourself, they will put you in a mental hospital and on tablets and your life will be over. Is that what you want?"

This frightened me and made me go silent because after looking up mental hospitals, I became emotionally paralysed. After being harassed and manipulated for two weeks by my father, I signed onto Job Seeker's Allowance because I wanted the abuse to stop.

Once I was signed on, I realised that I would need to write what jobs I had looked for and my advisor would then get in touch with the places to check that I wasn't lying.

My father argued with me and abused me verbally after I told him that I wouldn't lie.

He said something like, "Just do as I tell you and I mean what I say! They will not find out you are lying because I have been doing the same! I don't look for jobs, I write them down and I have gotten away with it!"

Have you ever felt that feeling where you know you shouldn't do something yet to save yourself from being hurt, you will do what you're told to do? This is how I was feeling and I carried on living each day like it was the same. Nothing would change apart from the date because the time would just go around in circles.

I signed on at the Job Centre twice, and on my second meeting, my advisor booked me in for a review which would help me in understanding what other jobs I could look for. I had only written Motor Vehicle technician because I studied it in college.

That was my only option which I could think about. Even though I did my year ten work placement at a supermarket, I couldn't see myself stacking shelves. How could I? I was depressed, not looking after myself and had no strength to carry on because my father didn't stop emotionally abusing me and the benefits which I was receiving was being taken by him.

To wake up each morning was a living nightmare because lifting the duvet off myself felt like I was lifting a ten ton weight. By the time I would lift the duvet off me, I would feel so exhausted, so I would just stay in bed for an hour before getting up. When you are depressed and you tell someone that "you're tired," they won't understand what you mean unless they have experienced it also.

The day of my review arrived, and I had to be there for 2:15pm. As someone from the internet company was coming to the house in the morning to fix the internet problems, I woke up early.

We got talking as he was fixing the problem and it seemed like I didn't feel as broken. It felt like I would enjoy the review later that day and I could stay positive even though I wasn't looking forward to the day.

Once the internet problem was resolved, we said our goodbyes before he left. I got changed to make myself look presentable for my review. Even though it wasn't a job interview, I wanted to make the effort. I looked at my phone as it gave me a notification that someone had texted me. I felt a sharp pain in my chest as I thought for a moment that it could be my father?

"If you have one hundred pounds in your account, then put in mine because we need to pay the mortgage. Ask your mum for bank details. You know your eldest brother is to blame," my father texted.

My mother came upstairs, and I asked her for the bank details while explaining what my father had written in the text. She looked at me and you could tell that she wanted to say something yet she didn't. After my mother gave me the bank details, I experienced a deep realisation which brought me to a conclusion. I read over the text one more time and then became so angry!

"You know what? I will not give the money! I can't take this anymore! If I am not back by 8:00pm, then don't wait for me!" I said to my mother.

"Wait! Don't go anywhere! I will phone him now!"

She went downstairs and raised her voice to my father over the phone.

"Why did you ask him? Why didn't you ask me first? Look what he is saying!" she said.

I went downstairs and my mother convinced me to speak with my father. I was so angry at her too because she never stood up for me when I needed her and because of this, I felt so vulnerable.

"If I ever start drinking or go on drugs, don't you ever blame me! I said to my father.

"It's okay, son. Don't worry, son. You don't have to give it. We will figure it out."

I handed the phone back to my mother, and she got off the phone. She walked behind me and told me to cancel my appointment and to just stay at home. I didn't know what to do because I was too hurt to think. All I knew was that my father would raise his voice once he got home. I went upstairs and phoned my advisor.

"Hello, it's Shikesh. We have a review meeting later on at 2:15pm. I would like to cancel the meeting because I have been abused as a child, so I am not fit to work. Please take me off benefits."

"Okay, that's fine and I am sorry to hear that. There is another benefit which you can claim and you will still receive money if you're not fit to work. Do you have a pen and paper?"

I wrote the number before my advisor wished me good luck. I thought to myself that I wouldn't claim benefits because I didn't want to have money as I knew my father would take it from me. Once I canceled my appointment and signed off Job Seeker's Allowance, I sat down for a few minutes to think.

"Monday 28th November 2011 isn't going to be a nice day," I thought to myself.

If my father cared about me, then why didn't he tell me about other benefits where I didn't need to work as I wasn't well? My father has been off work in the past where he has still claimed benefits, so he knew what support I could have.

"Hello, I would like to claim Employment and Support Allowance please," I said.

"Are you claiming any other benefits?"

"I have signed off Job Seeker's Allowance today and as I am not fit to work, I was told that I could claim Employment and Support Allowance."

After thinking about my situation, I signed onto Employment and Support Allowance because even though I didn't enjoy claiming benefits, I knew that I needed money to survive. Claiming benefits seemed like the only safest way in that moment for me to live another day.

Once I got off the phone, I stood up and started walking around the room while singing which made me cry. I needed to release some emotions, so it felt like singing helped. While I was walking around, I found myself facing the window and looking straight ahead. It felt like everything that I had experienced wasn't for nothing because there was a reason.

I then felt so much strength which helped me realise what I needed to do by thinking, "I want to know why I was given this life and why I suffered so much even if it kills me! In order for me to know the truth, I need to get help. Once I find the answers, I can then decide if I want to live or die."

Instantly, I picked up my papers and walked to my room to put them away in my wardrobe. While closing my wardrobe, it felt like I was frozen where I couldn't move. I then thought, "If I don't get help now myself, then I won't be able to get help at all."

Without thinking about anything else, I went back into the room that I was in and dialed 999.

"Hello, which service do you need?"

"Ambulance please," I replied.

"Okay, what's the problem?"

I started to cry. "I am suicidal and need someone to come and get me."

"Aw, what's the problem darling... why are you so upset?"

"My father has been emotionally abusing me for money and I can't take it anymore."

"I am sorry to hear that... where are you right now?"

"I am at home, so I am not a danger to anyone."

"Do you have any weapon with you?"

"There is a pair of scissors and a praying knife in the table draw in the room but I am not holding anything."

"An ambulance is on the way and they will be there within ten minutes, so I will stay on the phone with you until they get there."

The way I broke down over the phone to her while explaining why I was feeling suicidal, it felt like my final cry for help.

The doorbell rang. "There are police at the door," I informed the lady over the phone.

"Yes, I sent the police also because in this situation, the police always reach the scene before the ambulance."

"Oh, okay. I will just answer the door then."

I walked downstairs behind my mother as she gave me an evil look. "Did you call them?"

"Yes," I replied.

She became angry. "Why did you call them?"

My heart was beating so fast because after being silenced for so long and living with a fear of being sent to a mental hospital, I found my voice again!

I opened the door and there were two police officers outside.

"Hello, are you Shikesh?" he asked.

"Yes, I am."

"We were told to come here because you're suicidal. Get off the phone, so we can speak with you."

I thanked the lady over the phone for helping me and we said our goodbyes as she wished I felt better. Every minute that went by felt like an hour! The time went very slowly from that moment and it felt like I was dreaming because I was in complete shock of knowing that I had finally called for help. Somehow, I felt that everything would be okay.

We walked into the living room and sat down.

"Can you tell us what has been happening?" the police officer asked.

I started crying again. "My father has been emotionally abusing me for money and I can't take it anymore."

My mother then got off the phone to my father, so she walked into the living room while making excuses for her behaviour and my father's behaviour.

"He has done so much wrong and when he gets home, he will raise his voice at me again," I said.

"When I am looking at you, I see you're depressed, stressed, you haven't slept well, you haven't been eating well and you look really tired," the police officer said.

To hear those words from the police officer's mouth meant so much because I was reassured that people would understand what I had been experiencing and I wouldn't just sound like an attention seeker as my father had made me believe.

The doorbell rang, so one of the police officers stood up to answer the door.

The paramedics arrived. "Hello, I am just going to take a few details and check a few things before we take you to the hospital."

"Okay, that's fine."

I had to explain other moments where I tried to take my life and felt scared for a moment as I still had the fear of being sent to a mental hospital, so I left out the incident which took place a few months before Monday 28th November 2011 where I tried to get a knife from the kitchen to take my life and my father stopped me.

I talked a little, and we all laughed as I explained the exact time when my youngest brother would be at home which made it funny.

"Hello, did you enjoy school?" The paramedic asked my youngest brother once he got home.

He smiled. "Yes."

"You don't have to worry... your brother is okay," the paramedic reassured my youngest brother.

I then walked out of the house behind the paramedics and once I stepped outside, I looked around and saw school children walking by. It felt like I wasn't in my body and I wondered if what I felt was the same feeling that I would have experienced before dying?

"How are you feeling?" the police officer asked.

"Still not okay."

We then said our goodbyes as both police officers wished me better before I walked into the ambulance and sat down. Once the paramedics were ready, we were on our way to the hospital.

"Using headphones wasn't a good idea, was it?" the paramedic asked.

"No," I nodded.

I wasn't sure what to think about his question and whether he was telling me that my methods weren't affective or just comforting me? He then sat in the front passenger seat as I reflected on the day until that moment.

I thought, "I wonder how my review meeting would have gone? Why did this have to happen?"

After a short journey, we arrived at the hospital. I walked out of the ambulance and walked towards the side entrance as I saw a lady strapped to a stretcher who had just arrived at the hospital. A paramedic was pumping her chest, and it made me realise how close I was to taking my life. I never stopped thinking about that moment and just hope that she lived.

"You can go through that door and wait in the waiting area. Someone will call you," the paramedic said.

"Okay, thank you."

Before being able to think about how I felt, a doctor called me into the room.

"Hello, Mr. Sorathia. I need to check your blood pressure. So, what has been happening?" he asked.

I took a deep breath and somehow I didn't cry, not even a tear! I explained what had happened and why I was feeling suicidal that day. He was writing it down and taking it all in. After speaking to him, I waited in the waiting room again as a psychiatrist would examine me.

I looked at the clock. "I wonder how my review meeting would have gone?"

I hadn't thought about what I would have done until a week before that day. I wanted to make sure that if I was to take my life, then it involved maximum damage where I wouldn't survive.

The only thing that I could think about was jumping off a tall building. I wonder what would have happened if I had walked out of the house that day with the intention to take my life, because it wasn't just a plan anymore, it was about doing it.

I wasn't hungry, so I ate nothing all afternoon and just drank water at the hospital. As I had a lot of time to calm down and come back to reality, I didn't feel as emotional even though I was so tired. I waited at least four hours which felt like forty-eight hours until someone approached me.

"Are you Shikesh?" he asked.

I stood up. "Yes, I am."

"Who came with you?"

"No one... I came alone in the ambulance."

He looked around with concern on his face. "Okay, don't worry. Come with me, please."

We walked into a room and there was a table and chair at the front with another chair close to the corner of the room on the other side. It made me feel like I was a danger to someone while sitting in the corner of the room.

I then understood that it was for his and my safety in case I had severe psychotic mental health problems. The psychological examination then began.

"How often do you want to hurt people?" he asked.

I was confused. "What do you mean?"

"How often do you want to hurt people?" he asked again.

"Do you mean how often I want to hurt other people?"

"Yes."

"I don't want to hurt anyone! I don't even want to hurt the guy who abused me! I just want to hurt myself because I can't take it anymore!"

"Okay, please calm down. Tell me what has been happening?"

"Would it be better for me to tell you what I have experienced from my birth until now... It will make it easier to understand?"

"Yes, okay, say it like that then."

My whole journey of nineteen years was being shared, and I still didn't cry. I am uncertain about what he said before asking me for my father's mobile number. He asked me if I had anywhere else to stay and once he knew that I didn't; we agreed I would go home after the examination.

He was concerned because my father caused the problem, so if I was to be at home, then I may have been tempted to hurt myself. I reassured him that I could control myself because I wasn't feeling how I was in the morning.

"Hello, Mr. Sorathia? I am a psychiatrist calling from the hospital and have just been speaking to your son, Shikesh. We take very seriously what you have been doing. He will be coming home, so don't talk to him about money when he gets home. The well-being service will be coming to your house this Thursday."

The psychiatrist then asked me if I would go home by a taxi or I would like my father to pick me up? My father had always made me believe how every taxi driver was involved with the "paedophile ring," so I shouldn't use a taxi if I ever needed to get home because they would take me somewhere and hurt me. This is what I thought which made me tell the psychiatrist to ask my father to pick me up.

The psychiatrist then walked me out of the hospital as I thanked him. I waited outside of the hospital, so I would know when my father would arrive and while standing outside, I saw a gap between the stairs and thought of jumping. Even though I had calmed down, I still couldn't stop thinking about the abuse that I had experienced for so many months because the pain was still alive.

I thought, "How will he act towards me when he picks me up?"

After a short wait, my father arrived.

He had a smirk on his face. "Well, son, what can I say?"

I remained silent through the whole journey and as my youngest brother was sitting in the back, I didn't want to argue. The journey home was very intimidating as my father behaved like it was my fault and if I did nothing, then I wouldn't have been in such a situation?

My father didn't listen to the psychiatrist because as soon as we got home, he provoked me.

"Look, I made one hundred pounds today, so if you had given it to me, I would have paid you back. The psychiatrist saying they take things seriously... I take things seriously!" he said with an evil look while standing with his hand in his pocket.

All I could do was look at my father while saying nothing because I felt so traumatised. I decided to sleep, so I made my way upstairs.

"Where are you going?" he asked with a raised voice.

Once he saw me walking upstairs, he remained silent. I got in my room and just looked at my bed. It felt like I knew that something would happen that day because I made my bed in the morning which was something that I hadn't done for a while. After changing my clothes, I laid in bed and fell asleep after an hour.

It was around midnight when my mother woke me up.

"Your dad is calling you," she said.

I went downstairs. "Your eldest brother hasn't come home, and he isn't answering his phone. We are going to report him missing at the police station, so let's look for a recent photograph and then go."

He could have gone to the police station alone because instead of allowing me to go inside with him, he told me to stay in the car. The only reason why he took me was because he wanted no one to damage his car. Instead of allowing me to rest, he made me worry the whole night where I only slept for three hours.

The following morning, my mother woke me up again.

"Your dad is calling you," she said.

I walked downstairs while thinking, "what is he going to say now?"

My father shook my hand. "Let's have a fresh start."

He always told me not to tell the doctor about what I had experienced and was still experiencing because he believed that the "paedophile ring" had members working at the GP – General Practice. He always told me how if I told the doctor what I was experiencing, then they would pass the information to the gang and that's how they'd be able to hurt me more through witchcraft.

As my father wanted me to trust him again, he made me believe that he wanted to help me.

"Your mum will go with you to the GP and see what they can do about your sleep problems. Don't tell them what happened yesterday and before because they will do nothing," he said.

After visiting the GP, my father gained back my trust. As I look back now, I understand why my father denied me medical support. It's because he wanted to make sure that he never got caught and even though the psychiatrist knew what he had made me experience, my father's real agenda wasn't known.

Thursday 1st December 2011 had arrived, and I woke up early as I knew that the well-being service were coming.

I thought, "What will they say?"

My father was treating me like I was so important. The way he behaved and spoke to me, it made me believe that he realised what wrong he had done. It felt like he had learnt his lesson which made him finally start treating me like a son.

The doorbell rang, so I stood up to answer it.

"Hello, how are you?" the well-being service asked.

I let them in. "I'm okay thank you and you?"

"We are fine thank you."

We all walked into the living room and sat down.

"As you know, we are the well-being service and have read about what happened on Monday, so we just want to talk to you about it and see how we can help you further."

"Yes, that's fine. I was aware that you would be coming."

"Can you tell us what has been happening? they asked me.

I couldn't understand how I didn't cry at the hospital and when I was asked the same question at home, I cried so much?

"Ask him… ask my father… ask him… ask him…"

"He's been abused, and that's why he is feeling upset."

I cried more after hearing my father's reply because I knew why I was suicidal and he knew too. The well-being service then asked my parents to go upstairs, so they could speak with me alone.

"Now that it's just us, you can tell us in your own time what has been happening."

I explained what I had experienced since the start of 2010 and from the information that I shared; they knew I was suicidal because of emotional abuse from my father and not because of other reasons that my father had given.

They reassured me how strong I was to share my pain and how I wasn't to blame for how I was feeling. After hearing how I wouldn't be sent to a mental hospital or put on tablets, I was able to breathe.

"We will have a meeting when we get back and see what the right support will be. You will hear from us this evening to update you and if you need to speak to us, then you have our details."

I smiled. "Thank you so much, it means a lot!"

My parents then came downstairs once the well-being service had left. My father asked what was said, and I didn't tell him everything because even though he had my trust back, it would take a lot more than just a handshake for me to be okay with him.

After speaking to the well-being service that same evening, I was reassured again that I wouldn't be sent to a mental hospital or given medication because my situation had made me suicidal and nothing else. We discussed counselling as the right support and after discussing what I could do if I felt suicidal again, we said our goodbyes. Once I got off the phone, I went downstairs.

I gave my father an evil look. "They said I won't be put in a mental hospital or on medication. Counselling might be the support."

He looked at me while showing little interest in how I was feeling and more interested in whether I was still receiving benefits.

"That's good then if counselling will be given… are you still on benefits?"

"I signed off JSA and onto Employment and Support Allowance."

"So, you're on that one now?"

I wasn't sure what to think and was a little confused from how he spoke to me. Six days after the well-being service had visited, my father began emotionally abusing me for money again. He would also harass me and tell me to wake up early even if I got no sleep.

My father would say things like, "I will leave early and I want you to tell me which neighbour left and when. I will follow them, kill them and then claim self-defense."

He would also accuse me for bringing "unnecessary trouble" towards him such as getting help for myself to recover from being suicidal. As I look back now, I am not sure why I didn't tell the well-being service about how my father began treating me again. It may have been because I didn't care as I was still suicidal.

2012 had now begun, and I was still waiting for the phone call which would confirm the support that I would be given. After a month or two of waiting, I got a phone call to tell me that I had been put on a waiting list for counselling. I agreed to attend as I was ready to do whatever it took for me to break away from what I had experienced and find the answers of why I had to live through such abuse?

During the wait for another phone call which would confirm my counselling slot was available, my father didn't stop telling me about his plan to harm the "paedophile ring" because they were to blame for how my life was? He also made me believe how my grandmother was sucking my blood through witchcraft and that's why I couldn't eat?

When there would be a Hindu festival, my grandmother would stand in front of Gods statues and loosen her hair. She would then say words while moving her hands back and forth. After a few minutes, she would let out a loud scream while clapping her hands and turning around in a circle. My father believed that this was because she was calling an evil spirit inside of her.

There was a time at the start of 2012 when my father beat my grandmother on two occasions because he believed that she was doing witchcraft to the whole family. My mother was telling him to stop, and he didn't listen. Instead, he told my mother that he would beat her too if she told him to stop.

I became very frightened of my grandmother because my father brainwashed the whole family by making us believe how my grandmother could kill us by looking at us? Anytime I would walk past her, it would feel like I was going to have a heart attack because of how scared I was.

My father was also telling the whole family to loosen every screw in the house and apply a rustproof spray. He had met a guy in college who also believed in witchcraft and this is how he got the idea.

My father would say things like, "Demons like to sit on metal, so if you apply a rustproof spray, they will leave you alone."

It wasn't too long until my father admitted that it wasn't true and his friend who gave him the idea must have been crazy? Whenever we needed to use the bathroom, we would use a cloth and not let our hand make contact with the door handle.

My father would say something like, "Your grandmother is casting spells on the door handle, so whoever touches it will become unwell."

My father made me believe that I was being controlled through witchcraft because I didn't believe in what he did and if I wasn't being controlled through witchcraft, then I was a witch or the Devil himself.

My father also believes that when all of his kids including myself were conceived, there was an evil spirit inside both of my parents, so they may not be my parents spiritually.

April had now approached and my counselling slot became available. I was looking forward to it while not knowing what to expect. Before attending my first session, I assumed that my counsellor would tell me what to do which wasn't the case.

My father stopped taking my money, so it helped by knowing that I could plan for my future. Every time I came out of my counselling session, I felt like a King! My DJ career became my focus and while coming out of the darkness, I spent time with my music equipment once again.

My counsellor told me that by eating junk food, it would allow me to stay full and after a few weeks, I would feel hungry for healthier foods. I only weighed one hundred pounds, so I was eager to put on weight.

Until my second to last counselling session, I would have so many clothes on because I didn't want to look skinny. Even though I knew that people could tell how skinny I was by looking at my face, I felt less self-conscious by wearing more clothes.

This was a huge step for me because I had to accept how I looked and no matter how many clothes I wore, it needed to stop. I also understood why I enjoyed having long showers. After experiencing sexual abuse, I didn't feel clean most of the time, so by having long showers; it made me feel clean and pure.

Whenever I wore blue jeans, I felt so suffocated and this is something which I also understood in my counselling sessions. The family friend who abused me, he always wore blue jeans, so anytime I wore them; they reminded me of what happened.

I wasn't comfortable around guys, so this was also a big step for me. I never enjoyed being around guys and always wondered why I felt secure around girls in high school. After discussing this with my counsellor and by understanding how much the sexual abuse had affected me by both guys, I built up the strength to not let it affect my life any longer.

After attending five sessions, I wasn't feeling happy about my last session because I thought that it would be an ongoing support and not just a six session process. There was a lot of reflection and my counsellor handed me a referral to a place which would help me with my eating.

"I don't think that I will go to them," I said.

"Why not?"

"My eating difficulties isn't because of a medical problem. It's because of my situation. I will give myself a year and if I haven't put on any weight in that time, then I will go to them."

After discussing my counselling journey with my counsellor, she wished me good luck as I thanked her for the support that she had given to me.

The support that I received helped me with understanding my thoughts and emotions where I realised why I felt so broken. It allowed me to talk about what I had experienced which brought up so many lightbulb moments. The biggest thing it helped me with was to understand that I wasn't the problem.

I knew that my journey of recovery would not be easy because my father was still talking about his plan and telling me how I needed to harm the "paedophile ring" otherwise I wouldn't be safe.

After I completed my counselling, I spent the next two months doing nothing apart from thinking about everything that I had experienced until that day. I hadn't reflected on the past few months, so I did just that during the two months.

"Your grandmother isn't a witch, I was wrong. The whole world is so bad outside and no one will help you." my father said.

I didn't believe him in the end because I reassured myself from remembering the support which I had received.

Saying goodbye is never easy yet when you have to say goodbye to someone who you thought was a danger towards you, you become uncertain on how to say goodbye.

My grandmother wasn't eating or moving a lot for the whole day, so my father called an ambulance in the evening of Tuesday 7th August 2012.

After being seen by doctors once she got to the hospital, my father was told to prepare himself for the worst.

I got woken up early the following morning where my father, my eldest brother and myself made our way to the hospital. I remember the whole journey there which felt like it would be a goodbye. It was a very uncomfortable feeling and one that I will never forget!

We were standing beside my grandmother's bed when the same doctors approached us. The way they talked, you knew that there was little hope because my grandmother passed no urine for a few hours which confirmed that her time had arrived as her body was slowly shutting down.

I remember standing there and just looking at the urine bottle with so much anger while hoping that it wasn't her time just yet. Even though my father had made me believe such evil about her, I didn't want to believe any of it in that moment because it wasn't the way that I wanted to say goodbye to her.

After a short while, I called my mother to tell her to make her way to the hospital with my younger brothers. We all sat around my grandmother's bed before my father asked me to take my younger brothers downstairs and give them something to eat.

After thirty minutes, my eldest brother called me to tell me not to bring our younger brothers upstairs because the nurses were doing something. This is where I felt that my grandmother had passed away.

After ten minutes, my father came downstairs to make some phone calls and once he got off the phone, we all went back upstairs. My grandmother was lying flat on the bed with all of the pipes removed.

"She passed away," my father said.

He then sat down while looking at me. "How much money do you have?"

"Over one thousand pounds."

"We will need all of it."

I felt suffocated. "Okay."

He wouldn't take advantage of me during such a sad time, would he? The emotional abuse started all over again where my father was telling me to sign up to credit cards and loans also as he wanted as much money as possible from me.

I told my father that I wouldn't take out any loans or credit cards because I wouldn't go into any debt for him. I had already given him money which covered the deposit for the funeral, a plane ticket and a ceremony for my father to carry out in India because he was taking my grandmother's ashes back to where she was born.

The way that my father emotionally abused me, he didn't leave me a penny. I had several arguments with him because he didn't allow me to even have ten pounds. He made so many excuses to make me feel bad and tried to brainwash me with so many scenarios which made little sense.

"Your eldest brother paid for your tuition, so this is why I am taking it to pay him back," my father said.

"If my eldest brother paid for my tuition, then why didn't you sit us down and ask him if he wanted me to pay him back? If he said yes, then I would have paid him back in that moment!"

When I paid the deposit for the funeral, my father told me how it felt like a billion pounds had landed in his lap because he wouldn't have been able to handle the humiliation of not having money to give his own mother a funeral.

Once we attended the funeral and my father was back from India, I stayed in the house for a whole year.

I thought to myself, "He is taking every penny, so I can't even look for a job because I have no money to travel. Why doesn't he want to leave me with ten pounds even? I will make the most of my time inside of the house."

Staying inside of the house for a whole year wasn't a complete loss because I researched career options. The focus over my DJ career faded away because of the emotional abuse so I let it go.

There was a time in 2011 when I came across Life Coaching and realised that it was a career. I researched about it more and being self-employed was always a dream of mine!

While researching about Life Coaching, I came across a free counselling website where I listened to people and it touched me how they hadn't ever talked about their pain before to someone, yet they felt safe enough to open up to me about it even though they hadn't ever met me before?

I experienced a lightbulb moment. "What if Life Coaching is what I am meant to do?"

As the emotional abuse escalated from my father, I became suicidal once again. I was aware that if I needed any further support, then I would have to visit my GP. Being put on medication and on a waiting list for more counselling didn't appeal to me, so I chose not to go down that path.

The self-counselling and self-coaching approach became my savor because the help had to be instant and as I had built strength over the past few months, I knew that I had the emotional resilience for it. I also thought about paying for counselling and as I had no money, it was out of the question.

I thought to myself, "My approach to helping people is very unique because it is self-taught from personal experiences and not something which I have read from a book. What if I was born to help people and everything that I have experienced, it was needed to give me the empathy and everything else needed to change lives?"

I now welcomed 2013 and when I thought things couldn't get any worse, I was wrong!

My father asked me to sit down with him as he held a book in his hand. "I have been reading this book and just realised why we had so much pain in our bodies. There are holes under the wall and this neighbour has been releasing carbon monoxide poisoning from his gas fire place. This is why we have had so much pain for so many years."

I took a deep breath. "So, witchcraft isn't real?"

"It is… I have three theories now. Witchcraft, poison in our food which people were putting in when we were not at home or carbon monoxide poisoning from this neighbour."

Walking upstairs to sleep felt impossible that evening because it seemed like when I would have the smallest of hope in achieving my dreams, something would knock me down and it was always because of my father.

Before my father became a gas safe engineer, he was fixing the boiler at home himself and by doing this without being qualified, he has broken the law several times. He would spend all day trying to fix it even though he had no idea on what to do.

During this time, I questioned my father about it and he denied ever doing anything wrong. I am not a plumber and do not know about boilers, what I do know is that nothing is ever fully safe.

Throughout 2013, I kept myself occupied with research to plan for my future and also spoke to people online. Even though I didn't have a real social life, I didn't feel all alone because I was communicating with people even from a distance.

I still felt very vulnerable and didn't know what support was available which would allow me to move out of the house. Finding support wasn't always my concern because it seemed like being suicidal was a yearly event for me.

During December 2013, my father told me to give him more money after promising not to take anymore from April 2013. At first, I agreed because I stopped caring and didn't want the trouble as I was unwell.

I thought, "When is this going to stop? I have to put a stop to it for good!"

In the evening, I got into a big argument with my father where my mother joined in and she explained how hurt she felt whenever he took money from me.

"I have been thinking about going back to college yet you haven't given me the chance!" I said to my father.

"When have I stopped you? I haven't stop you doing anything!"

"You are taking every single penny from me! I have had so many arguments with you to stop taking my money, but you don't even leave me with ten pounds in my account! You promised you would not take any more after April 2013 yet here you are telling me to give you four hundred pounds! I am twenty-one years of age and I need money too! I have a life too!"

It felt impossible to not think about death because I was so hurt and didn't know what would help me to calm down. My father stopped me from doing fireworks which I had saved for New Year's. I assumed that noise and colours in the sky would distract me but I wasn't given the chance to find out.

This was the only time I used alcohol to cope with an emotional situation because I wanted to fall asleep and not think about how broken I felt. All I could think about was taking my life and as I was drunk, my emotions escalated.

The next morning, I sat on the edge of my bed as I thought, "I could choose crime to live, I could take my own life or I could change my life for the better?"

After mind mapping the decisions that I had, I gave myself forty-eight hours to decide on one and if I couldn't decide between that time, then I would have taken my life. By realising that I wasn't able to cope without alcohol, I remained alert about my well-being.

My father was aware of how desperate I was to have my money back because all I wanted to do was live my life. He would always promise to pay me back and I wouldn't receive anything. I even told my father to not speak about my past because it made me feel like giving up and he wouldn't listen.

The times when I looked for work, I felt so angry because I didn't even have the strength to stack shelves and I felt helpless by even thinking about it. My confidence and self-esteem were at its lowest and even though I could speak, I still felt silenced.

Before forty-eight hours were over, I decided on what I would do and from the decision that I made; it changed everything! While making my decision, I thought, "I need confidence and self-esteem to find a job. This will help me to save money and move out."

The pain that I felt by thinking about going back to college was unbearable and it was a feeling that I didn't want. Even though I disliked the thought of going back to college, I knew that it was essential because if I wanted to achieve my dreams, then I had to do something which I didn't enjoy.

I looked through the courses on the college website and seemed to always read through one particular programme. It felt like someone was shining a light over it and telling me that it would change my life. There were moments where I laughed at myself because I assumed that I needed ten years of therapy to overcome my past, so what would twelve weeks do?

As I knew what my plan was, I was committed to doing whatever it took to change my life, so if I achieved nothing at the end of the programme, then I wouldn't have lost anything.

When you have been controlled for so long where you have had to ask permission for everything, you fall into the same cycle because after deciding to go back to college; I asked my father if it was a good idea? Even though he agreed that it was a good idea, I still felt held back by his response because I didn't want to ask for his permission about anything ever again!

They say that the first step is always the hardest, and it's true! Every time I picked up the phone to bring a positive change into my life, it took a lot of strength for me to do so.

The taster evening for the programme was either at the end of December 2013 or the start of January 2014. During the taster evening, we played a game of who could build the tallest tower, getting to know each other and then sitting down to share our reason for wanting to attend the programme.

All I heard was complete silence and to realise that everyone were listening, it felt great because for most of my life; I wasn't heard at home. I also informed everyone that I was going on the programme while being suicidal and I wasn't expecting to be supported in the most caring way that I was.

The taster evening then ended, and it was time to leave. It was a cold, dark and windy evening where I walked home the whole forty minutes. All I could do was smile because I kept experiencing a very warm feeling inside of my heart as I knew that everything was going to be okay.

After a few days, I went back to college to fill in the application form to enroll myself onto the programme. I don't think that I have ever been so stressed to complete an application form in my life!

The reason why the application form was so difficult to fill in was because I needed to provide information about the counselling that I had attended at the GP. As my college welfare officer wasn't aware that I was joining the programme, she didn't disclose any information when my team leader asked her.

My only option was to go to the GP and ask my counsellor about talking to my team leader. The visit was a waste of time because she wasn't there anymore and the doctor that I was seeing to get sick notes from, he also wasn't there! I felt stuck and didn't know what to do which made me feel like it would have been better to take my life as it seemed easier.

Something kept telling me to keep going, and that's what I did. I went to college to hand in the other forms which I had already filled in and while I waited for my team leader in reception; I questioned myself if I should have just left and given up?

It seemed like I was signing up to fail with how stressful it was of not knowing what to do. Once my team leader walked into reception, I handed her the forms and told her that I wasn't able to speak to my counsellor or the doctor because neither of them were at the GP anymore.

After speaking with my team leader, I made my way home and once I changed my clothes and sat on the sofa; I experienced a lightbulb moment which made me realise that I could find my counsellor online, so I turned on my laptop and began my search.

That very second, I took my phone out of my pocket and dialed her number. It rang and kept on ringing. After a few more seconds, someone answered.

I had a lovely conversation with my counsellor about how I was doing and what I was up to. I also told her about my achievement in putting on weight and it felt great to hear her response. She then wished me luck before we said our goodbyes. Finally, things were back on track!

During the early weeks of 2014, I received a phone call from my team leader to inform me of my place on the programme. Hearing those words felt like listening to a song which you can't get out of your head! I looked up testimonials of people who had completed the programme and I cried because I knew that everything would get better even though it would not be easy.

I kept telling myself to keep going and not give up because something amazing would happen at the end of the programme. It was towards the end of January 2014 and I didn't sleep well the night before as I was both excited and nervous about my first day on the Prince's Trust Team Programme.

Even though I wanted to stay in bed, I didn't forget how hard it was to get on the programme, so I told myself that I would not give up without trying. The first week of the programme was all about getting to know each other and making meal plans for our residential trip the following week.

I knew that I would be okay from day one of the programme because my team leader's genuine and caring approach made me feel important which was something that I didn't experience at home. Being at college felt like a real home because I could be myself and when it would be time to go home, I would become silent again.

My father didn't make things easier for me because when I would arrive home, he would have me sit with him and tell me the same conversation of going after the paedophile ring. He would make me believe how I still had to hurt them because that was the only way for me to live? Two hours would go by and he would still be talking!

We all know how taking a break to recharge is essential because it gives us a clearer mind and time to reflect. This is what I experienced during the residential trip on the second week and before I left, I told my father that I would try to message him if I could while making no promises. Deep down, I knew that I wouldn't message him because he was the last person that I wanted to speak with.

Not having any contact with my father for a whole week gave me more than just reflection. It gave me peace; I spoke with others, my happiness became my importance and I ate even more where I also grew taller. My team leader noticed every small change that I was experiencing and always reassured me by telling me that she was there if I ever needed to talk.

The first three weeks of the programme felt impossible and not just because of my father, it was also because of how much my legs ached. As I had remained in the house for a whole year, I had to teach myself to walk again. Sometimes, I walked to college and back home because I knew how much exercise my legs needed.

The programme for me wasn't just about gaining confidence, it was also about working towards putting my past behind me. Before joining the programme, I told myself that I would get all the help that I could because I wasn't willing to feel the same way at the end of the programme.

Sometimes, I felt like phoning my team leader and telling her that I wouldn't complete the programme because it was too hard. The one thing which I didn't forget was how emotionally resilient I was and if I could phone an ambulance and then enroll myself onto a programme, then I could complete it. This gave me the strength to walk into college every morning before class began.

It was in February 2014 when I visited the college counsellor the first time which was another person from who I was seeing in 2010 and 2011. I knew that there were only twelve weeks in the programme, so I had to make the most of every day!

My college counsellor could see that I needed support from the quick chat that we had, so he booked a session for me to see him again the following week. Waiting for something is what I have always disliked because each day feels like a whole month! All I could do was stay calm and wait for the following week to arrive because I couldn't force the day to come any sooner.

The day of the session arrived, and it was at lunch time, so I hurried to the canteen and ate. I couldn't stop thinking about what would happen and whether I would feel better or worse? I even told myself to not go because it would have been easier. Once I finished eating, I walked up the stairs and approached the room before knocking on the door.

I waited patiently. "Hello, I have a session booked with you today," I said.

"What time is it booked for?"

"It's booked for 12:30pm. I came to see you last week, and you booked a session for me today at 12:30pm."

"Okay, don't worry. Come in and please take a seat."

I went over my life story to help him understand what I had experienced and how it had made me feel for so long. I shared things which I had told no one as it felt like it was the right time to talk about it.

From attending the session, I learnt two things which changed my perspective and allowed me to let go of so many negative emotions, feelings and thoughts. The first thing was that my eldest brother abused me because he wanted to and not because of witchcraft. The second thing was that my mood swings were caused from what my father was making me experience and not because I was the problem.

Before the session ended, he showed me a diagram to help me understand what my father was making me experience. I had never seen it before and wasn't sure what I was looking at until he explained what a drama triangle is.

I went home that day with a big smile because I experienced a breakthrough in understanding what was happening. Before I went to sleep that night, I sat on my bed and told myself that I didn't need to worry about anything because whatever I was experiencing, someone was making me experience it which was out of my control.

This was the first time in a long time where I slept through the night and felt so rested when I woke up the following morning.

PERSECUTOR

RESCUER   VICTIM

A drama triangle is a diagram which shows what happens when someone has control over another person. The person being controlled wouldn't know why they would be experiencing so many mood swings until someone tells them. To help you understand this better, I have included a scenario below of what I was experiencing.

Scenario: My father emotionally abusing me for money.

My father playing all three roles:

Persecutor: If you don't give it, your brothers will become homeless, is that what you want? You better listen because I mean what I say!

Rescuer: I am doing this for you.

Victim: I am sorry, son, I don't know what to do. People are after me and I had no choice.

I would be made to play all three roles:

Persecutor: I will not give it to him again! Why do I always end up giving it to him? I need to say no and stick to my answer!

Rescuer: It's not his fault because he's doing it for me. If he didn't take it, then I wouldn't be safe, and he only wants the best for me.

Victim: Why do I keep giving it and why do I keep falling in his trap? Why can't I stop it? What am I doing wrong? This is the last time!

Things were now looking up, and I felt more positive. I talked more in class and it didn't bother me if anyone found me to be annoying. I knew why I was talking a lot and that's all that mattered. My team leader was so shocked at how fast I had progressed and when we would have our one-to-one meetings, she would express how amazed she was by seeing me so confident at such an early stage in my personal development.

There was a time during week three or four of our community project where we were waiting on some materials to be passed for safety. As we had to wait for the paperwork, we stayed in class and my team leader thought that it was best to try an activity which she hadn't done before.

It's called the stress box exercise, and the aim is to rip scrap paper, scrunch it into a ball, say what has been making you feel overwhelmed and then throw the ball in a small box. This would continue until everyone has expressed themselves. After this, everyone would go around the table and pick up each ball from the box while saying what they are grateful for. The main outcome of this exercise would be to replace negativity with positivity.

Everything was going well until I became emotional. I cried, and it felt like I couldn't breathe where you could hear the hesitation in my voice. After some deep breaths, I said what was on my mind.

Before this moment, my team members had never seen me emotional and weren't aware of what I had experienced. After seeing the way I broke down, they realised how vulnerable I was which made them understand how hard each day was for me.

It felt like we all became closer as a team because we shared personal details during the exercise and understood each other better. This was the turning point for me to become more outspoken and not hide away any longer.

It seemed like my aim to help people was becoming a reality because we all had to give a presentation on a topic of our choice. I thought about so many topics from music to rollercoasters and wasn't sure what topic I would choose in the end.

I was thinking about what I wanted to do in my life and how much I wanted to be happy. It seems ironic when I think about it now because the topic that I gave my presentation on was success.

You needed to be there to experience what happened because it felt like I was teaching! I gave ideas to my team members of what they could do with their interests and how they could turn them into a career!

I also included a diagram of a stairway to success and when my team leader realised that I had designed it myself, she couldn't believe it as she thought that I had taken an image from the internet.

Even though it was just a presentation, for me it felt like so much more because I was made to feel worthless for so long and now I felt like I was taking back more control over my life. This was something that I wasn't able to do before.

There was even a time where my team leader had put me in charge of the whole class for the morning and I had to make sure that every task was completed before lunch time. At first, I felt like I couldn't do it and was so nervous because I had never taken charge of a whole class before! After this experience, I told myself to keep saying yes to opportunities because I wouldn't know what I can achieve if I don't accept the challenge.

I also delivered a safeguarding workshop on the four categories of abuse which are emotional, neglect, physical and sexual. This was possible with the unconditional support from The Victoria Climbié

Foundation UK where I did my two-week work placement while on the programme.

While planning for the workshop, I was asked to come up with as many questions as I could about abuse. I came up with one hundred questions in total! This proved that anything is possible and when there are no limits to success, you will be amazed at what you can achieve if you really put your mind to it.

It was coming to the end of the programme and with three weeks remaining; it was time to break a record with my team which wasn't planned. Weeks ten and eleven were all about team challenges and this is where we had to give back and do something within our community. The record which was held were six team challenges, so my team and myself broke that record by completing seven team challenges!

I remember that exact moment when we had completed six challenges where we felt how amazing it would be to hold the record and as we still had two or three days remaining before the final week, it would be possible.

During one of the team challenges, a team member, and myself were making our way to a museum to plan a sponsored walk and I wasn't looking forward to the travelling. As I wasn't used to travelling alone, reading the London tube map felt like rocket science. This was the start for me to travel alone with confidence.

The final week now arrived and the planning for the final presentation had begun. My team members and myself had to write a speech which we would give during the final presentation in front of family, friends, work placement staff and others. As I was now aware that my parents didn't care about me, I didn't invite them.

The only people who came to support me that I knew outside the programme were my college counsellor, the programme director of The Victoria Climbié Foundation UK and her daughter who I met on the day.

A lady who did her social work placement at the foundation couldn't stay as she had to be somewhere, however, it still meant so much to see her even for a few minutes.

The presentation had now begun, and I had already done my bit during the first half of explaining what each week was about. My role was to speak about week nine which was next steps where we worked on our CV and learnt to write cover letters. I was so nervous and glad that it was over because I wasn't used to giving presentations in front of so many people.

After the first half, we had a short break, and I didn't want to think about what would happen next because I wasn't sure how I would get through giving my speech. I could feel my legs shaking and how nervous I was which made me decide to give my speech after three of my team members so I could then stay seated.

Below is my speech that I gave in the final presentation:

Before I joined the programme, I had no confidence at all and by being suicidal at the same time; it was either that I take my own life or I change my life around for the better. I chose to change my life around as I wanted to be different from the people who have hurt me in my past and not turn into a criminal as choosing crime was an option which I once thought about.

I haven't had the best of lives however who does? We all come from different paths and we all have experienced and witnessed many different things which some we are able to relate to and the rest, we can only imagine of what it would be like for us.

I already knew about the Team programme as I had been searching up courses and also charities which may help me get to where I want to be. I was also looking to get into work, however, from the severe anxiety and the lack of confidence, I knew that I would become very stressed easily, so I had no choice but to go back to college even though I didn't like the idea. Sometimes, we have to do things which we don't like, however; the outcome is what will help us reach our goal in life.

I chose this programme as I felt that it was right for me. I did my research about the course by watching videos of people who had already completed the programme and listening to how their life changed throughout the programme and after. Once I had done the research, I was certain that this programme will help me get to where I want to be, however; I wasn't aware of how I would become a new person completely.

When I joined the programme, I was still suicidal and my confidence was at its lowest. I was also emotionally broken and mentally damaged. As I had pushed myself out from my comfort zone, I became very tired easily as my sleep routine was a complete mess. At times, it felt like the world was falling on top of me and this lead my mind to thinking that I should leave the programme and drop out. I knew that I had to keep a positive mind as when you are recovering from falling down, the first step will always be the hardest.

The first three weeks of the programme were very hard for me as I wasn't sure whether I would be able to complete the whole twelve weeks or not, however, after the third week, I began to change my thoughts as I had a wake-up call from knowing that I am slowly getting there and I am much more than what people made me believe in the past.

Throughout the programme, each week gave me more confidence and boost. I learnt new skills and gained more knowledge. Not only did I become happier, however, I was able to slowly put my past behind me. At times, I may think about it only to help me learn how not to make the same mistakes which I once upon a time made in the past. I became more out spoken where I was able to share my views and also my experiences with my team members and team leader freely.

Not only did I understand myself better, however, I stopped blaming myself and feeling guilty for the things which were not my fault. I engaged more in team activities and throughout the course; I was also able to be a leader for the first time where I achieved what was set out to be completed by my team leader.

I also had a chance to put together a workshop and to deliver it to my team. This was the first time that I had done this and I have to thank my work placement for giving me that chance. I have to thank my team leader Shareen for introducing me to the foundation as without her, I wouldn't have had the chance to go through this experience.

It was not only a work placement; it was an eye opening experience where I am now at peace with my own life. I believe that things happen for a reason and nothing is a coincidence.

Before I joined my work placement, I came up with a quote which helped me understand things in a whole new dimension. On the day that I started work experience, my employer Stephanie was going to tell me that I am not a victim, so I shouldn't tell myself that, however, I took the words right from her mouth just by saying these words.

"I am not a victim, I am a witness, so it is my duty to give a testimony in order to eventually heal lives and stop abuse."

Once I had spoken those words, Stephanie looked at me and said that I was just about to talk to you and explain this, however, you already came prepared. I agreed with her as we both smiled.

By the end of the programme, I became a new person who was filled with confidence and boost, who was able to speak freely, who was able to take up challenges and complete them, who was not only able to move on from the challenges that he once faced in the beginning, however, he was also able to feel positive about himself.

There are so many things which I have learnt and will take away from the programme. One of those things is that you should not say no to a certain task or challenge which is introduced to you.

Before, I used to say no to anything which I felt I was not good at, however, if we keep saying no, how will we find out whether we have that skill or not? Saying no is a sign of fear and the best things normally come with fear. We should learn to say yes because we won't know what is behind the closed door until we open it and step inside.

We are normally scared of failing, however, is it really failing? I believe that no one is a failure as we just didn't get to the end. If we are really determined about something, then we can reach the finish line. We learn new things and become better at our skills which we hold. Not getting to the finish line the first time just means that we were not fully ready. We can always get there the second time.

This programme which I call journey has been more than a twelve week development programme. It has been a life changing experience which has brought out the real me. Before, I never had the confidence to talk in social situations, I wasn't able to cope with my emotions which lead my mind to destruction quite easily. By going through this twelve week journey, I now have all of the tools, guidance and skills to help me with my future and to reach my life goal.

Before the programme, I knew that I wanted to inspire and empower people by listening to them and giving them guidance using various techniques to get people thinking and for them to realise the truth and not to live in denial.

I have now decided to become a mentor for young people and to help them achieve the best that they can in their lives and then around ten years down the line, I wish to become a certified life coach and become self-employed as I have always wanted to be my own boss where everything is flexible for me.

I am now able to be mentally and emotionally strong as talking to the college counsellor Paul has woken me up from how I used to think. He has helped me to stop living in denial. He has taught me many different things and if it wasn't for him, then I don't think that I would be able to understand each situation and handle the present and future problems which I may face, so for that reason, I want to thank him with all my heart and I hope that he achieves everything that he has planned for himself in the future. He is an amazing man and a light which shines bright.

I would also like to thank Shareen, Emilie, Benson, Nicci, Ewan, Alisha, Anastasia, Alka, everyone at The Victoria Climbié Foundation UK and all of my team members for helping me achieve so many things throughout the programme. I wish all of them the very best and the greatest success in their lives. I also want to thank Sherna who was my counsellor in 2012 at the GP when I was not in a good place at all. If I have missed anyone out, then I do apologise.

Before I finish my speech, I would like to leave you with some inspirational philosophy which I came up with in business terms. I came up with this during the last three weeks of the programme and this is how it goes.

Your life is your business and your employees are the people who are close to you and may know you quite well or very well. Some of them will just be in it for the ride which maybe because of the name that you have or the things that you own. Some may just be in it because they want something from you, however, they are not there when you need them the most.

Having these sorts of employees would bring down your business and keep you thinking negative. You might even think about giving up on the things which you really want to achieve in life. You need to sack these sorts of employees and get rid of them for good. You need to then employ new people who will make your business a success by helping you and keeping your mind positive. Once you have done that, you will then see how amazing your life really is.

Thank you for listening and I hope you enjoyed my speech.

I couldn't understand how I only had one tear in my eye and not more? It seems like the strength that I had built over the twelve weeks; it allowed me to remain emotionally resilient on the final day which made me stay calm even though there was a point where I felt like crying my eyes out.

It was now time to go home, and I wasn't concerned about what my father would say because I felt so relieved by knowing that I had completed the programme! For the first time, I did something with my own will and not because I was made to do it or found myself in a situation which I was pushed into.

There was a time during the final week where my team members and myself had planned to give our own gifts to our team leader. I sat next to my team leader as I watched her open everything that my team members had got her and felt terrible for not getting her anything. I am not sure what my team leader thought about me not getting her a gift and I know that she wasn't able to understand why.

The reason why I didn't give her a gift is because no matter what I would have given her, it wouldn't have been enough to say thank you for how much she supported me. No matter what I thought about getting her, it didn't make me feel like it would say what I wanted it to say. The amount of support that she gave is priceless where no matter how many times I will thank her for how much she did for me, it won't ever be enough!

Thank you so much Shareen for all of your support! If it wasn't for you, then I wouldn't have been able to complete the programme and also have further support after.

I reflected over the twelve weeks of how broken I was at the start and after twelve weeks of so many amazing achievements; it felt like I experienced a spiritual rebirth. My future was now my main motive, and I was empowered to work through my progression plan which I did with my team leader.

This is where I thought back to a conversation that I had with my college counsellor where he guided me around the next steps. My options were to complete Counselling Skills Level Two and then if I wanted, I could complete Counselling Studies Level Three. I was certain that I wouldn't become a counsellor as I needed the practical element and not just listening and questioning, so I decided to complete Counselling Skills Level Two and then a Life Coaching course.

One thing which I have learnt about planning is to keep all options open because you never know what will happen from one day to the next. It's also important to stay open-minded because it can feel like things will work out in the way that you may have visualised your plans, however, in reality, it's not always the same.

As my counselling course would start in September, I decided to volunteer at The Victoria Climbié Foundation UK. After visiting them and having a meeting, I waited until they had a plan set out. I also got in touch with The Prince's Trust to enquire about volunteering as a Young Ambassador.

It seemed like everything was going to plan until I realised that the counselling course which I signed up for wasn't the full course. This made me believe that my plans were being pushed back. If I wanted to do the full course, then I would have had to wait a year.

I looked online for places near me which offered the full course and I am so glad that I did because I found a place which offered the full course and at a much cheaper price! I wanted to make sure that I had my place reserved, so I called them up to attend an interview.

By attending the interview, I realised something which would have changed everything for the worse if I had enquired about the course in 2011. If I was still in therapy and/or very vulnerable, then I wouldn't have been allowed on the course as it would have been too much for me to cope with. I felt so relieved by not enquiring about it in 2011 because I was so close to losing all hope.

I now started my voluntary role at The Victoria Climbié Foundation UK where I worked on two projects. One was a safeguarding workshop which was delivered to the team after me on the Team programme and the second was a summer project for young people.

My team leader had expressed her thoughts of wanting me to deliver a safeguarding workshop again as it was so powerful the first time. The second time I delivered the workshop, it was meant to last two hours and ended up lasting four hours which had to be continued with another day. I learnt two main things after this experience.

The first is that I needed to learn the skills of keeping in time no matter how much needed to be done and the second thing that I learnt was that safeguarding needs to be talked about a lot more because for a workshop to go over by two hours, it proves that a lot needs to be said by so many people.

I had never put together a summer project before and didn't know what it involved. This is where I learnt the ins and outs of what goes into the planning of a project and how much work needs to be done.

It was the final day of the summer project and I couldn't be there as I had an interview at The Prince's Trust for the Young Ambassador role. The interview was very powerful as I had to share my story once again and by the end of the interview; it felt like I took back even more control over my past and to deal with it in my own way and to not listen to my father any longer.

I realised that when you talk about your past more than once; you break away the control which it has over you and once the control is broken, it will never affect you again no matter how many low moments you may experience in your life.

I had now completed my voluntary role at The Victoria Climbié Foundation UK and began my Counselling Skills Level Two course. I also received a phone call from The Prince's Trust who congratulated me for being given a voluntary opportunity as a Young Ambassador!

From not being certain of how things would develop for me in order to move onto the next stages of my life, everything felt amazing because for once, it felt like I was walking on the right road. I completed my Young Ambassador training and was now waiting to attend my very first event which would be at the start of 2015.

It was December 2014, and I imagined a scenario where my eldest brother would be holding my child in the future if I kept speaking to him. I didn't understand what caused this scenario to develop. As I look back now, it seems like the breakthrough which I experienced during the counselling session in college; I was reassured of knowing that he was guilty and not innocent which is why the scenario affected me so much.

That same evening, I was sitting downstairs and watching TV when my younger brother said something abusive towards me which triggered the scenario that I was thinking about. I felt so much anger and looked at my mother while she was reading the newspaper.

"Next time my eldest brother phones, tell him that I want nothing to do with him!" I said.

"What did you say?"

"You heard what I said."

She walked into the room that my father was in and told him. He asked to speak with me and made me pour my heart out before emotionally abusing me and making me feel like whatever happened to me, it wasn't important.

"What about them, haven't they hurt you?" he said.

"They have hurt me and they will suffer in their own way!"

"Why didn't you speak when you were little?"

I took a deep breath. "Both of you were always arguing. You beat her so bad on so many occasions where I was so scared of you and I kept thinking that you would hurt me if I was to tell you. You had already told me how you would chop me into pieces and throw me in the garden if I was to go against you."

My father has asked me the same question of why I didn't speak about the abuse when I was little and every time I have explained the same reason, he has denied being responsible for keeping me quiet.

"I now have one question for you and tell me the truth. Why did you tell me that you would throw me in a skip and drive away at such a young age when I asked you when you would take me bowling?" I asked.

"I was experiencing car crime and couldn't take you. I wanted you to stop asking me, so I thought it was the best way by telling you what I told you."

"You think that was the best way... to tell a child such a thing? Are you serious right now?" I stood up to walk out of the room. "I want nothing to do with you as well."

After thirty minutes, my father walked into the living room and sat down on the sofa next to me.

"I think you should reconsider your decision because it wasn't his fault for what he did to you. He also doesn't remember what you told him about the abuse. I told him to lie, and this is why he told you he remembers," he said.

Have you ever felt so traumatised that you couldn't speak? Even when I wanted to scream, I couldn't open my mouth because I felt that traumatised. All I wanted to do was die in that moment because it felt like my life was that worthless.

Not only did my father emotionally abuse me that evening, he also thought that it was best to tell me how he didn't listen because he felt that his agenda was more important than mine. For four years, I was made to believe that something could still happen about the first abuse case when really, I was made to live in false hope and the times I asked my eldest brother if he was ready to tell the police, he would confirm that he was yet he never told me what the truth really was.

My eldest brother was aware of how I wanted no lies in the investigation because I have always been about the truth. He was old enough to know between right and wrong and the path that he took was to keep lying to me while taking advantage of money from me!

The following morning, I had my strength back, so I made my way downstairs.

"Why did you lie to me?" I asked my father.

"I wanted to make things easier for you, so that's why I lied to you."

"I told you that I wanted no lies, so trying to make things easier for me is out of the question. If I didn't say anything, then I would have understood, but you knew that I wanted no lies and you still went against my words? I experienced the abuse and not you or him!"

"Why are you trying to break the family apart?" he asked with an evil smirk on his face.

"How am I trying to break the family apart? You are the one who is breaking the family apart by lying to everyone and doing whatever you want! You have never listened to me! Instead, you have always just hurt me!"

I became suicidal once again and as I had accomplished so many things throughout 2014, I knew who I could turn to if I needed support. This is where I experienced a lightbulb moment and realised that I didn't need to work with young people and then become a Life Coach because I was already prepared for it.

By knowing that I was ready to become self-employed once I had completed my courses where I could then offer youth coaching as a service, I didn't feel as broken because I now had a lot to live for by remembering how many people had supported me. This allowed me to keep my hope in humanity as I knew that everyone isn't evil.

2015 had now begun and while still feeling suicidal, I attended my first event as a Young Ambassador. I remember waking up that day and just lying in bed after getting dressed and thinking if I should have jumped in front of a train to end my life? It seemed like a good idea because I didn't want to carry on being hurt anymore.

Like several times in the past, I put on a fake smile and got on with the day. This is how I coped for the next three months before I started to feel alive again.

It was a good balance for me of volunteering as a Young Ambassador which would involve two to three events per month and also attending my Counselling Skills Level Two course in the evening. What I wasn't expecting was to experience another transformational journey! I also had to keep a journal throughout my course which my tutor would read and this made me feel like someone was listening.

For once, I had a lot of support around me and this kept me going because it wasn't 2011 anymore; it was 2015 where I had so much to remember to become emotionally resilient once again!

My father was still harassing me because he would drop me off and pick me up after my class. During the journey, he wouldn't stop talking about my past and there was even a time where he parked his car in a carpark just to show me some damage which he felt was important for me to see? It wasn't anything different from what I had already seen in the past, so it seemed pointless. Even when I suggested for him to take a picture and to show me at home, he didn't listen.

I always tried to keep a clear mind to focus on my course because I wanted to pass it and not fail. I didn't want to retake the exam again when I could put all the work in and pass the first time.

My father always made things hard for me and even when I asked him to let me concentrate on my work, he would raise his voice and tell me how I was telling him that his life wasn't important. This would make me feel helpless because it felt like I was always being accused by him for something which wasn't my fault.

Being told about his plan to commit a crime never helped me because I kept thinking that if I needed to go to prison to be safe, then what was the point for me to even plan for my future?

I was also blamed for the way his life was including his failed attempts at fixing his own car. When I was a teenager, he used to take me to a car park and have me stand outside in the cold for over two hours. There was a time where I almost lost a finger and he still didn't care.

He would say things like, "Just shut the... listen you piece of... you need to sort your pathetic life out... I've paid for your clothes, your driving lessons, your tuition and everything else, so why do you have a problem with me taking your money? You must have the devil in you... you're a witch... some people need to look after their own agenda."

After nine months of hard work and pure dedication, it was time to find out whether I had passed my Counselling Skills Level Two exam or not. I was so nervous and felt sick to my stomach by thinking how I may react if I didn't pass. I knew how terrible the feeling of failing was and it was something that I didn't want to experience again.

We were all sat down and waited for our tutor to start the class.

"I've just received the exam results and you have all passed!" she said with a big smile.

I was speechless. "Do you mean that every single one of us has passed?" I asked.

She smiled even more while confirming that everyone had passed. The relief that I felt and the stress which I had experienced for the past nine months left my body! I felt even more hunger to achieve my future goals because from everything that my father had put me through during my course, I still passed!

I went home that evening and was over the moon. The feeling which I experienced after completing the Team programme was nothing compared to what I felt after passing my Counselling Skills Level Two course. Even with the chaos that I was living in, I still managed to keep my focus and not go off track!

I want to thank my tutor, my classmates and everyone at the centre for supporting me throughout my course. You all helped me in achieving my qualification and for that, I will always be so grateful and will never forget any of you!

My search had now begun in looking for a Life Coaching course and I came across one which was being offered by the same awarding body of the counselling course that I completed. There was a Level Three and a Level Four which I would need to complete, so I picked up the phone to enquire. As there was no answer, I left a message.

I soon realised that I would have to wait a year because there weren't enough tutor's available to deliver the course that same year.

I thought about what I could do because if I had to wait a year, then I could look for work and save money. After evaluating all of my options, I decided to look online for another Life Coaching course and this is where I came across the same one which I was looking at in 2011.

It was an online course and I could email my tutor my assignments. There was no exam at the end, so it was a guaranteed pass! I could also send in the assignments whenever I wanted, so there were no deadlines! At the end of the course, I would be ready to become self-employed.

The only way I could make sure that the course was for me was to have my questions answered by phoning the office. I now had the confidence to talk over the phone and also ask for help, so I wasn't shy or afraid to speak any longer. After having my questions answered, I knew what I needed to do.

Another thing which I have learnt about life is that you should take every opportunity which arrives and evaluate what can be done now and what can be done in the future. There was an event from The Prince's Trust where I could go on a boat trip for a week or start my Diploma.

The date that I had decided to start my Diploma on wouldn't have been possible if I went on the boat trip, so I had to make a decision of what felt right. I started my Diploma in September 2015 on a specific date as I wanted to take control over it and give it a meaning which would last where I wouldn't feel so broken when thinking about it any longer.

Tuesday 22nd September 2015 was my twenty-fourth birthday and on this day, I started my Diploma. My birthday always made me feel like I was born into a life which I didn't choose and I wanted to give it a new meaning where I chose the reason for how my life would be from that day onwards. This was the main reason for choosing my birthday as the start date for something so beautiful!

I had now been a Young Ambassador for twelve months which was an incredible journey! I spoke at many events and came across so many incredible people with such powerful stories to share.

What I wasn't expecting was a phone call about an event where I could judge the awards. The Prince's Trust do an awards ceremony each year called Celebrate Success for all of the programmes that they offer.

What made it even more worthwhile was when I found out that I had been nominated and then shortlisted for the Young Ambassador of the Year Award! I had to choose someone to be my second champion, so I asked someone that I knew and it felt amazing to hear her excitement!

It feels like yesterday as that's how well I remember it. It was Wednesday 2nd December 2015 where my friend and myself made our way to the venue. We spoke the whole way there and reflected from the first moment we spoke. As we had arrived a little early, we went into a café close by.

It had been a whole year since we had seen each other and within that year; I had put on more weight which made me look even healthier. It felt great for it to be noticed because finally; I didn't have to pretend to be someone else by wearing so many clothes.

Once everyone had arrived, the show started and each category of the awards were being called out. There were live performances also which was a new experience for me as I had never seen a live band before, so to experience it was amazing!

It was now time for the Young Ambassador of the Year Award and I was up against two other guys who I had known from start of my Young Ambassador role. Before our names and stories were shared, we wished each other the best of luck.

I could feel my legs shaking as my heart raced and for that moment, nothing else mattered! Everything went silent and if a pin was to drop, then you would have heard it. The envelope was now being opened, and that moment became so intense! I kept thinking, "It couldn't be me, could it?"

"And the winner is... Shikesh Sorathia."

It felt like I wasn't present in that moment because it was just a dream. It took me a few seconds to realise what had happened and before I stood up to walk on stage, I looked over to both of my friends as we shared a silent moment and smiled.

I got handed my award by a gentleman from Mappin & Webb as we shook hands before I was interviewed by AJ King from Kiss FM.

"So, how does it feel?"

"Well, my hearts beating, so…" everyone laughed. "Um, but it feels amazing, absolutely amazing. I mean, just a year on where being suicidal, but still wanting to live and now on a stage holding an award. It's… it's surreal."

"Brilliant, brilliant and… and what are your plans for the future?"

"Well, right now I am in the middle of my Life Coaching Diploma, so next year, I'll be self-employed coaching other people in personal development to change their lives, so…"

"Brilliant, truly positive… round of applause… that's really good… really good… really good."

Both of my friends were then invited to the stage and before we went backstage to have our pictures taken and for our comments to be given to the press, we were handed our certificates.

It felt great to meet new people and to also catch-up with so many others who I had met during various events. When you're surrounded by so many people who genuinely care about you, you realise how lucky you are and no matter what might be happening in your life, it becomes a tiny problem.

I want to thank Robin for nominating me for the award, being my champion and always being there. My friend, thank you so much for always supporting me, being my champion and recording the moment when I received my award. Lastly, everyone who supported me and helped me in realising my full potential, thank you so much!

There was only one thing left to do that evening which was to go back home to where I felt like an outsider. When you have achieved something, you would be so excited to go home and celebrate it with your family. Even more so, you would want your family to experience the event with you.

I was fully aware at this point of how little my parents cared about me, so they were the last people I would invite. I felt suffocated when I got back home because I knew how unloved my parents made me feel. When my father held his hand out to hold my award, I wasn't going to allow him because of how much abuse he had made me experience.

I gave him a third and final chance and I hoped that he would realise what he would lose, if he didn't stop emotionally abusing me and controlling my life, so I let him hold it.

For a few months during 2015, a stray cat used to walk into our house and leave after a few minutes as the garden door would be open. This became a regular occurrence, so my father looked after her. She was covered in fleas and the times my younger brothers told my father to take her to the vet, he would say things like, "I don't want to in case the neighbour owns her... a pet isn't just for Christmas, a pet is for life."

There was even a moment where he approached me and told me that if I was man enough, then I would look after a cat in my life? I did nothing to cause such a reaction and I couldn't understand what made my father say such a thing? Was he talking about himself and as he didn't want to carry the pain, he thought that it was okay to give it to me and make me feel worthless?

Instead of taking the cat to the vet, he was asking my younger brother to research about it and buying flea killing sprays. It became a very depressing situation and there was a point where I felt suicidal because by seeing my youngest brother's body covered in flea bites, I felt helpless.

It was one evening in December 2015 when I went downstairs to eat. My younger brothers told me that the cat was locked in our neighbour's garage and they couldn't do anything because our father told them not to knock on the neighbour's door.

I wasn't speaking to my father and as I knew how manipulative he was, I stayed away from him and didn't react. Thirty hours later, the cat was still in the neighbour's garage, so my father called the animal rescue team before backing up a copy of the CCTV. He was saying things like, "If he hasn't let the cat out by the time I have finished backing up the CCTV, I will kill him."

While waiting for the animal rescue team, the neighbour came out of his house and walked towards his garage while carrying a bucket, so I ran upstairs to see what he was doing. Once the cat saw an escape, she ran out of the garage and jumped through the window into our kitchen.

My heart raced as I ran downstairs and sat on the sofa. I looked at my father and felt such anger because whatever his agenda was, he made everyone else experience such a traumatic event. It seems like he doesn't care about animals either from the way he treated the cat.

I used to love the thought of having pets before this experience and after experiencing such pain from it, I decided that I wouldn't have any pets in the future. It took me a long time to let go of the pain because I couldn't feel peace when thinking about it. Thankfully, I have slowly let go of the pain and if I have any pets in the future, then I will give them so much love and care.

After a few days, I was sitting on the sofa with my younger brothers while our mother was standing.

My father approached her and said, "For a few days, I will not eat or drink anything from you."

"What is the reason... tell me... what is the reason?"

"There is no reason, I just have to do this."

Once my father walked out of the living room, my younger brother looked at me and asked, "What is his problem?"

"I don't know?"

It was the 30th December 2015 and I couldn't fall asleep as I heard my parents arguing, so I sat on my bed and I couldn't believe what I had heard. My mother was speaking with a raised voice and I could hear everything.

"Before you go, make sure you do the brick wall!" she said.

"I won't be doing it."

"Then who will do it if you won't be doing it?"

"Shikesh will do it."

She sounded confused. "Shikesh will do it? Shikesh won't do it... make sure you do it before you go!"

I became concerned because I couldn't understand why my father was telling my mother that I would do the brick wall? I had no such conversation about it with my father, so why did he believe that I would do it? He had ordered building materials as he wanted to remove the fences in the front and back garden to put a brick wall, so once he was in prison, my mother would get the full price of the house after selling it.

It was confusing because my father would say things like, "Once I am in prison, your mum can sell the house and you all can move to a new place and live happy... you need to go to prison also otherwise you will be a coward and not safe around this paedophile ring."

The following morning while I was pouring milk over my cereal, my mother came downstairs and wanted to speak.

"Shikesh, do you have a stomachache?" she asked.

"No, I don't... why?"

She cried. "He said I put poison in the food and now your little brother got a stomachache. He blamed me I make him ill, and I did nothing. He threatened me he will divorce me and call police for me one time in this house after he takes my eyes out and he will make me beg in the street."

"Okay, don't worry... don't cry. I am here for you and I will not let him hurt you, don't worry... watch what I do now!"

I walked to the front door and got hold of a baseball bat while my mother walked behind me.

"Shikesh, no... he's my husband!"

My father came out of the bathroom, so I let go of the baseball bat and approached him.

"Why did you threaten her? She told me how you accused her of poisoning her own son and then you told her how you would take her eyes out, make her beg on the street and also call the police for her... you got nothing to say, no?"

I walked into the living room and my father followed me after washing the shaving cream off his face.

"Look, I didn't say anything to her... she is lying!"

My mother cried louder. "I am not lying! You told me these words... you are lying and not me!"

"I said those words to other people and not you!"

"No, you didn't say it to other people, you said it to me... don't lie, you said it to me!"

I sat down on the sofa and told my father that I would report everything to the police. He twisted every word before sitting in front of me and pointing his finger at me.

He gave me an evil look as he said, "Listen to me now!"

"No! I am not going to listen to you! You have hurt me so much in the past, so you tell me, why should I listen to you?"

He looked at my mother and became furious as he pointed his finger at her. "After I have gone to prison, I will divorce you! I will finally give you a divorce!"

The way she cried in that moment, it felt like it was her final cry for help because I had never seen her cry the way she did.

I sat down at the dining table to eat my breakfast because I decided to go to the police station, so I needed all the energy. I couldn't take any more drama and just needed it all to stop.

My father convinced me to not go as he made me believe that he would hurt someone within two months and if I was to tell the police what was happening, then they wouldn't believe me as I had no evidence to prove it.

After cleaning up the cereal from the floor which I had accidently poured when my father tried to grab my arm to apologise, I told both of my parents that they needed to do something together because if a paedophile ring was after their kids, then for them to be parents, they had a responsibility to protect them.

"I agree with him, he's right," my father said.

Did I just hear my father agree with me for the first time? I wasn't sure what to think, what to say or even do because whenever I told my father to do the right thing, he never agreed with me, so why did he agree with me this time?

He then handed me three envelopes, and they all had a message on the back.

"Don't open any of them until I am in prison. Just read the messages on the back," he said.

The first envelope was addressed to my eldest brother, the second was addressed to the solicitor and the final one was addressed to me which said, "You have a BIG job Shikesh. Because your eldest brother isn't here anymore, you will look after the house and your younger brothers."

I couldn't understand what it meant, and I felt too traumatised to even ask about it. What could I have said in that moment? Why didn't my father talk to me about it directly? My father walked out of the living room and came back with a long copper pipe with a white pipe over one side. Once my father removed the white pipe, there was a knife stuck into one end.

"I will use this to kill the neighbour," he said before putting it back.

My father got afraid of me going to the police, so I gave him two choices. If what he was telling me was true, then he had to do something within the two months like he had said, otherwise, I would call the police and report everything.

As he didn't want me to go to the police, both of my parents got dressed and went out to make me believe that something would happen. After an hour later, they came back and had done nothing. My father looked at me with fear showing in his eyes.

"Give me two months and I will do something, I promise you," he said.

"You have two months and if you haven't done anything, I will call the police at this house."

"You won't need to because something will be done. I showed you the pipe and the knife which I will use. There are empty alcohol bottles which I have saved and will make petrol bombs."

Was I shocked to hear my father's response? No, because in the past when he would explain how he would kill someone, using a petrol bomb was one of those ways.

I didn't even know how to report it because the police would need solid evidence and as my father has gotten away from being caught in the past, he would have gotten again because he knew my intentions, so he was prepared for what may have happened.

It wasn't too long until he threw away the empty bottles and removed the knife, so if I had called the police, then it would have been my word against his and as he would have manipulated my younger brothers and mother in making them believe a false scenario, they would have said nothing out of fear.

If he could keep me under his control for several years, then he could have done it to both of my younger brothers also if he had no other way to look innocent.

In the past, he said something like, "I have two gallons of petrol in the garden. If the police were to search my house, I would tell them it's for the petrol lawnmower. Why do you think I brought a petrol one and not electric? They wouldn't be able to do anything because they wouldn't be able to prove me wrong."

By remembering this, I knew that my father had himself prepared for every circumstance which reassured me of how it would have been my word against his. This is how prepared my father has been to stay away from being caught and as he knew how to manipulate every situation, my voice wouldn't have been heard.

The New Year was twenty minutes away, so I got the fireworks ready. I was so excited to do them in the morning and after experiencing such a painful day; I wasn't excited any longer. My father rushed out into the garden as he wanted to light a rocket.

He felt that it was okay to come out only when he wanted and not be there from the start? It's understandable that he wasn't in the mood to celebrate, he should have thought about his younger kids at least.

Once the fireworks were over, I took off my shoes and felt that I needed to say something. It felt like if I didn't say it, then I would have regretted it, so I walked into the living room and looked at my father.

"I want nothing to do with you anymore," I said.

"Huh?"

"I want nothing to do with anymore. I will do something myself and I will then leave for good where you will never see me again and that's a promise!"

I turned around and walked up the stairs before stopping half way. "You know words spoken are like fired bullets, you can't take them back," my father said.

"Yes, well, I am being serious and I will prove it."

I got into my room and changed my clothes before sitting on my bed and thinking, "What just happened?"

What I told my father, it allowed me to feel relieved with no regrets. It felt like it couldn't be avoided and it happened for the right reasons. I felt happy inside and instead of experiencing negative emotions, feelings and thoughts, my body experienced joy because I weakened my father's control over my life.

Waking up the next morning felt amazing, and I carried on with life. After having breakfast, I was making my way upstairs when my father walked into the living room.

"All right, Shikesh?" he asked.

I gave him no reply and didn't even look at him. Even though I was motivated to carry on with my life and not give up, I became physically sick for two weeks. My mother was still vulnerable, so when she would sit next to me and explain how she was feeling, I would calm her down, so she wouldn't break down crying.

"He's playing with my mind… I'm not going to listen to him from now," she said.

"Okay, if you feel that he's playing with your mind, then you don't have to listen to him anymore. You can listen to your own mind. Don't worry about what he says, just ignore him. I'm doing the same thing."

It wasn't too long until my mother spoke to my father again and the way she behaved around him, it seemed like nothing had happened between them? I couldn't understand why my mother behaved in such a way because she began to make me feel like I was the problem?

Life at home was becoming unbearable, so I decided to get help from a housing officer. I wasn't confident about leaving home because I feared what would happen? What my father had made me believe was something that I was still thinking about.

As I didn't have any of my own suitcases, I ordered two of them, so if I decided to leave, then I would have something to put my clothes in. My father was at home the day they arrived, so he answered the door.

Once my mother came home, my father told her to ask me about my plans. The only times she would come up and harass me the way she did, it would only be when my father would tell her to get information from me.

"Where are you going to go... are you going to another country?" she asked.

"With what money? I don't know what I am going to do."

"It's not your father's fault, okay? He did everything he could."

"Really, he did everything that he could? Emotionally abusing me and taking my money from me? Yes, he sure did everything that he could, didn't he?"

"He will do something in two weeks now, so wait until then."

"He promised he would do something by the end of 2015 and he didn't, so why should I listen to his promises anymore? You were so hurt because of what he said to you and now you're acting like nothing happened?"

After my mother convinced me to wait for two weeks, she went downstairs to tell my father what I told her.

"He said, if you haven't done anything in two weeks, he will call the police," she said.

"I'll kill him first and then the rest!"

I couldn't understand what my father's real motives were because he would pretend to make me feel like he cared about me and from the way he spoke and treated me, it proved that I was the least of his worries.

After attending the meeting with the housing officer, my gut feeling was telling me not to go and the thought of living in a hostel made me feel so helpless. The same evening when I got home, I emailed the housing officer to tell him that I wasn't ready.

During the same week, I was sitting downstairs when my mother looked at me.

"Look, your dad is going to do something and go, I might have to also go, so you have to stay here and look after these children," she said.

I didn't know what to say and just needed to think, so I went upstairs to rest. The message which I read on the envelope that was addressed to me made complete sense! The lightbulb moment which I experienced in that moment made me realise what my father's agenda was and why he wanted me to stay.

Every time when I would ask for my money back, my father would tell me, "Once I am gone, all of this is yours, so what are you complaining about?" I wasn't able to understand what he meant until that moment when I experienced the lightbulb moment.

Waiting no longer, I walked down the stairs and stood in front of my mother.

"I am not going to take this responsibility because I can't even look after myself and I am trying to get my life together which I haven't been able to because he has been taking my money! You make sure that you understand this! I will not be taking this responsibility!" I said.

She spoke in a sweet voice. "Okay, don't worry. I will stay here and look after them, you don't need to."

The same evening when my father came home, my mother told him what I had said to her. It seemed like my father didn't care because even though he didn't say it to my face, I felt the desperation in his voice for wanting to make sure that I didn't leave home.

It was the final week of January 2016 and I completed my Young Ambassador role. Fifteen months had gone by and it didn't even seem that long! The evening of the celebration event felt surreal because I attended my first event during January 2015 while feeling so broken and here I was again feeling the same way while attending the celebration event at the start of 2016.

It felt so great to see all of the Young Ambassadors who I had met at the beginning and by seeing so many other people who attended to celebrate it with us; it felt really special.

All of the Young Ambassadors including myself had to give a speech at the end to share our thoughts on our journey before receiving our certificates. Whenever I gave a speech at an event, it was always without any notes or pre-rehearsing.

I would also use a technique to involve the audience and only when I felt it would have the most impact. I would ask the audience to close their eyes and then have them imagine being in a dark room where there would be no light. There would be sharp nails hanging from the walls and if they were to move, then they would get hurt. I would then have them imagine the words Prince's Trust where they would see a light shining through the keyhole.

This is what would open the door and once every young person would be out of the dark room, they would have so many people around them to support them and make them feel safe. During this moment, I would ask the audience to open their eyes and have them look around to see how many people would listen and help.

I shared this same technique at the Young Ambassador celebration event to show everyone how powerful words really are. Giving a speech is like taking the audience on a journey where you get to decide how they feel and what they see. This is the beauty in giving a speech because words don't just create emotions, feelings and thoughts, they create a live performance!

The happiness which I experienced at the event would not last because I knew what environment I was going back to. What made it bearable was the news which I received prior to the event. I was shortlisted for the Young Ambassador of the Year Award and would be attending the national finals!

I want to thank every single person who I met during my role as a Young Ambassador because without your support, I wouldn't have been able to complete my role and develop in every way both personally and professionally.

Two weeks had now gone by and it seemed like it would be another normal day where I would have to continue living with so much pain because my father didn't keep his promise of doing something. I freshened up and was all alone in the house which felt better than nothing as I didn't have to hear my parents' voices. For a few seconds, it seemed like Saturday 20th February 2016 would be a little easier.

Something then happened... something big happened! I dialed 101, a non-emergency number and spoke to a police officer.

"Hi there, I am not sure if I want to report this and before I do, I want some guidance around it. The first thing is about sexual abuse which I have experienced and the second thing is about carbon monoxide poisoning," I said.

"Okay, tell me about the sexual abuse first."

I explained the abuse from both guys and wanted to know what the police did with sexual abuse cases when my father had made me believe that my eldest brother wasn't to blame because it happened through witchcraft? As I knew why it happened, I needed to let go of it and the only way that I could do so was to report it to the police.

"The witchcraft, it's crap... don't believe it, okay?" he said.

"Okay."

I cannot remember what he said about the carbon monoxide poisoning.

Once I got off the phone, my heart raced because he informed me that police officers were on their way to the house to take a statement. It was finally happening! What I had been silenced with for five years would now be exposed! I waited for the police officers while thinking about the breakthrough which I was experiencing.

After waiting a short while, the doorbell rang.

"Hello, may we come in?" the police officers asked.

"Yes, please do. You can go through to the living room."

"Just so you know, we have our cameras on, so everything is being recorded."

"Okay, that's fine."

"So, why are we here?"

I had told my story several times during my role as a Young Ambassador, so it felt easy to talk about. Once the statement was taken, I asked if the carbon monoxide poisoning theory could be investigated and I was told that it would be too hard to prove, so they didn't take a statement.

After a few minutes, my parents and younger brothers arrived home. One of the police officers went upstairs to talk to my father before both of the police officers left.

My father came downstairs and sat on the sofa to take off his shoes while looking at me with an evil stare.

"So, you want to tell me what happened?" he asked.

I stood up and started to walk out of the living room. "No, I don't."

"That's fine... you do what you want, mate."

"I will."

After a few minutes, my mother was sent up to get information from me, so my father could stay prepared to look innocent. As I knew that he didn't care about me or my life, I didn't tell my mother what I told the police.

During the end of February 2016, I experienced something so powerful which brought everything into a simple conclusion. The reason why my father made me lie to the police when I was young was because he wanted to strengthen his cases that he was reporting to the police. He felt that the police would listen to him if he made up stories about his kids being in a serious danger.

The times when he emotionally, verbally and physically abused me as a child, it was to keep me living in fear and afraid of him which was the only way that he could make sure I remained alone and vulnerable. He only pretended to care about me which kept me blinded from realising that he was to blame and no one else.

By controlling my entire life since the age of seventeen, he wanted to make sure that I didn't leave home because it was the only way that he felt he could achieve his plan of revenge while knowing that I was at home looking after the house and my younger brothers.

He wouldn't have even told me about the responsibility unless he was in prison. He wanted it to seem like he was innocent and this is why he controlled my mind so much to not realise the truth. The moment he gave me the envelopes was only because he felt that he would do something that day, otherwise, he would have kept it a secret.

This is why he said things like, "If you have a girlfriend before I have done something, she will claim false rape charges as she will be paid off," to make sure that I had no one to support me because if I did, then I wouldn't have stayed in such a toxic environment.

Everything that my father said and did, it was to make sure that I was always at home and this was the real reason for his control over my life. He felt that his selfish plan would only work if I was at home because he had convinced my mother that she also needed to do something.

This was the only reason why he agreed with me on the 31st December 2015 because it's what he had planned. He never intended to give the responsibility to my eldest brother because he knew how selfish he was and not loyal. If he wanted to give my eldest brother such a responsibility, then he wouldn't have told me at seventeen years of age, "I thought you would look after your two younger brothers once I was gone, but I was wrong."

I was looking at myself in the mirror the whole time while experiencing this powerful awakening and it felt like someone was watching over me. I didn't know what to say or do and it didn't matter in that moment because after experiencing such a powerful awakening, I knew the truth! The peace that I felt during that moment is something that I can never explain because it has to be experienced.

After feeling spiritually alone for so long, I didn't feel alone any longer. I always knew that if I broke my silence about the sexual abuse by my eldest brother, then I would set myself free. By experiencing the awakening which I did, I knew that I was right. It wasn't just about the sexual abuse, it was also about breaking away from my father's beliefs because he made me believe how anything that I said or done, it was because of witchcraft and not because it's who I am.

While still sitting on my bed, I thought, "Why does he want to harm people and why is he blaming them for his life being the way it is when he is responsible?"

It was Friday 4th March 2016 when I made my way to the police station to give a video statement about the sexual abuse by my eldest brother. I had to get two buses, and I wasn't nervous at all. I reflected during the journey and still couldn't believe the powerful awaking which I had experienced. As I look back now, it seems like everything has happened when it needed to and the times I felt so alone; it was something that I had to experience to understand that I was never alone.

I thought about the first case in 2010 where I wasn't prepared because I answered with "probably" on almost every question. It may have been because I knew nothing would happen, so by giving the same answer, I assumed that it would make things easier?

When I got to the police station to give my second and final video statement, I was taken into a waiting room while everything was being prepared. It seemed like that little broken boy who felt so unloved at home, he didn't feel unloved anymore because the waiting room had a lot of toys and children's books inside. It felt like my childhood would be reclaimed and I wouldn't feel damaged anymore!

After a short wait, I walked into the interview room feeling so confident and emotionally resilient. It felt like I had broken away from my past already! One thing which I have learnt is if something is meant to happen, then it will happen so naturally where you won't even need to plan for it.

I made my way home after the interview and still felt so confident without a single negative emotion, feeling or thought taking me off track. I felt amazing, and I understood how important it is to put the past behind you because if you don't, then you will always feel trapped. Once I got home, I changed my clothes and carried on with my Life Coaching Diploma.

I woke up so early on Monday 7th March 2016 as it was the national awards event! After getting dressed in a three piece suit, I made my way to the train station and waited for my friend. We talked all the way through the journey until we got to the London Palladium where the event was being held. The first thing that we noticed was the red carpet, and it wasn't something which we would only see.

It was a little cold that day which didn't bother us too much. We waited outside and spoke to a few people before being allowed to go inside for an introduction. Walking on the red carpet felt luxurious and even though there was a lot of chaos in my life, I could still stay positive because deep down, I knew that I wasn't born for no reason.

I also destroyed a fear that day which had haunted me for so many years. I knew that this fear would be destroyed at some point, however; I wasn't sure when it would happen? For so many years, I felt like people were watching me eat and this made me feel self-conscious to eat in public.

Before the main event, we ate at a place close by to the London Palladium and this is where I ate a full meal in public for the first time without feeling self-conscious any longer! It seems like breaking away from my father's control allowed me to develop in every way.

After eating, we were making our way back and had to walk slowly because there was a huge crowd along the road due to the event. As celebrities also arrived, there was a lot of press outside.

"Shikesh!" someone called.

"Shareen!" I looked towards my friend. "It's Shareen!"

We couldn't believe it as we were speaking about her and saying how amazing it would have been if she was there with us. Another team leader from The Prince's Trust was also present, and it brought me back to 2014 when my journey of recovery began.

Once everyone were seated inside, we waited for one more person. I had never met him in real life before, so I was so excited to meet him. The trumpet played, so we all stood up and welcomed His Royal Highness, The Prince of Wales. It's quite something when you see someone on TV and then meet them in person.

The main event was very emotional because every story was so unique and you realise how precious life really is. It was great to see live performances also which allowed us to calm down from being overloaded with emotions and it's true, Ant and Dec are hysterical! The speech that His Royal Highness, The Prince of Wales gave at the end was both heartfelt and funny!

After the main event, we were at the after party and it was great to catch-up with so many people who I had met during my role as a Young Ambassador. Every conversation was emotional from remembering every event and I was then standing on the side while drinking wine before being approached by Helen Lederer! It's not every day where you get to drink wine with Helen Lederer and speak for over thirty minutes!

I learnt that winning isn't everything and even though I got an award for remaining a finalist, it still made me feel like I had failed? I believe that it wasn't meant to be because The Prince's Trust didn't know my full story as I didn't know it myself until a month before the event.

One thing is for sure, if I never star in any films, series, theatre, release any music in my life or win any other awards, then I will always remember what it felt like to be a star even for that one day!

I want to thank every single person who supported me on the day and cheered me on. All of you played such an important role in my life and I will always be grateful for how loved you made me feel.

It was now the end of March 2016 and I completed my Life Coaching Diploma. After so many weeks of wondering if I could complete it, I achieved it with a distinction!

Before starting any business planning, I took a three week break to get my strength back and to reflect on where I was in life.

During my three-week break, I received a phone call and I cannot remember the whole conversation because I was speechless from what I heard. It was the fortieth anniversary of The Prince's Trust that year and it would be celebrated at Buckingham Palace in the Royal garden.

From how much I had achieved both personally and professionally, I was recommended to take part in a formal presentation for His Royal Highness, The Prince of Wales where I would stand beside Sir Ben Kingsley and Young Ambassadors!

The event took place on Tuesday 17th May 2016 and from the start until the end; it was mind blowing! What made it even more worthwhile was that I had grown so much since the start of 2014 and was now confident to travel alone and eat in front of people without feeling the anxiety that I used to feel.

To be recognised for everything that I achieved meant so much because I wasn't being made to feel like I was worthless any longer.

Robin, thank you so much for always being there and making me feel important. I also want to thank His Royal Highness, The Prince of Wales and Sir Ben Kingsley for your kind words. Lastly, thank you to everyone as a whole for being there and making the event happen!

The day my Diploma arrived in the post, my mother answered the door and instead of giving it to me herself, she asked my younger brother.

I looked at him in disbelief while my mother walked passed me.

"What have I done to her?" I asked my younger brother.

My mother looked back and stood still. "What have I done to you?" I asked.

"You haven't done anything."

"Then why are you treating me like I have?"

"Look, I am worried about your youngest brother because he isn't well, so leave me alone."

"You are not treating your husband or anyone else differently, so why are you treating me differently? A mother never treats her children differently just because one of them isn't well!"

"You haven't done anything… stop asking me."

"Has your husband told you to treat me like this? He must have because you only do something when he tells you to do it. Is this about your eldest son and what he did to me?"

"Don't talk about it in front of your youngest brother!"

I went silent because she began making me look like I was the problem. It seems like my parents were so against my youngest brother knowing about the sexual abuse and how to be aware of how it happens to people?

They would tell both of my younger brothers similar events of what their families have done yet if I mentioned a word of it, then it becomes a crime in my parents eyes?

I couldn't understand why she would treat me like I wasn't her son? I can't remember how long after it was when I was alone with her at home. My heart raced as I walked down the stairs and once I approached her, she was sat on the bed with her back facing me.

"What have I done so wrong to you? You have been treating me differently and I want to know now! Don't give me the silent treatment when I haven't done anything wrong to you! Either you tell me yourself or I will call the police and you can tell me in front of them!" I said.

She stood up and looked at me. "It's your fault your younger brother lost weight and if he fails his GCSE's, it will be your fault!"

"Are you serious? You want to blame me when I did nothing and you couldn't even look at me? I am not to blame for anything and you know that, so why are you holding me responsible? If the sexual abuse case goes to court, then you will need to be there and I will tell the court how you treated me during the investigation, even when you told me yourself that my eldest brother is guilty because he wanted to do it and not because of witchcraft! You put your hand your heart and told me!"

She went silent again, so I went to my room to calm down. My mind was all over the place because I couldn't believe what I had heard. Without me doing anything wrong, she made me feel responsible and from the way she spoke, I knew that my father had a huge part to play.

After an hour, I went downstairs to eat lunch and my mother approached me. "Are you taking me to court?" she asked.

"If the sexual abuse case goes to court, then you will have to be there too."

"Are you going to start a court case just for me?"

"If you push me that far, then yes, I will take you to court. Do you think that you can accuse me of such a thing and I'm just going to leave it? I haven't done anything wrong to you and you turned against me for no reason! You begged for my help at the end of last year and now you're treating me like I am not your son?"

"Why did you tell your younger brother what happened to you?"

"He asked me why I wasn't speaking to my father and my eldest brother! I was planning to leave, and that's why I told him because he deserves to know the truth! Look at what lies have done to this family and your husband is to blame. I didn't tell him everything that happened, I just told him that my eldest brother abused me and benefited with money from me, so that's why I stopped speaking to him. You and your husband keep telling him about your families and how bad they are. If I tell him what wrong has been done to me and by whom, then it's a crime to you because you don't want him to know how I've been treated. You wanted to keep it a secret and make it seem like I was the problem when you, your husband and your eldest son are the problem!"

"I didn't know he asked you, I thought you told him yourself?"

"Why didn't you come and ask me then? You normally harass me and ask me about everything, so why not this time?"

"Your father told me to ask you, but I didn't want to."

"That's your problem then! You chose not to ask me, so you take the blame! Don't accuse me of things which are not my fault!"

"I didn't know... I didn't know..."

"That's the problem... you never know, do you? You just do it! The way you have been treating me is how a mother should never treat her son. You make food and then leave it on the table without telling me?"

"You have eyes don't you... you can see I've made it. You can take it yourself!"

"That's what I'm talking about. This is how you've been treating me. I know I can take it myself, but I choose not too because if you think that you can treat me in such a way, then I rather not eat any of your food at all. This is why I started cooking my own food and washing my own clothes because I don't need you anymore, especially after how you've treated me!"

She sat on the sofa and looked down.

"I have one question for you now. Have I ever done anything wrong to this family?" I asked.

I had to ask her five times before getting a reply.

She gave me an evil look. "No!"

"Just like him, I want nothing to do with you either from today onwards. You are dead to me!"

I walked out of the living room and closed the door behind me before going to my room. The same evening when my father came home, my mother told him what happened while I was upstairs and from the way she spoke, my father realised that I wasn't going to stay quiet and accept the abuse that both of my parents were making me experience.

He also corrected himself by understanding that my younger brother asked me why I wasn't speaking to him or my eldest brother and not because I told him myself without a reason. This is what my father has always done. He has formed his own conclusions without knowing the truth and then he would manipulate his own conclusion until someone has corrected him.

All my mother had to do was ask me and because she didn't, she pushed her son away who was always there for her. Whenever I looked at my mother after this day, I could see the guilt and loneliness eating away at her no matter how many times she pretended to be okay in front of my younger brothers.

When you have hurt an innocent person in the most evil ways, you can never get over the pain no matter what you may do. Even confessing won't bring you peace because the truth is that unbearable!

It was Friday 27th May 2016, and I was doing my business planning. My phone rang, and I wondered if it was the police to tell me about my case? As it was an unknown number, I didn't think it could be anyone else for that moment.

"Hello, is this Shikesh?" she asked.

"Yes… it is."

"I am a police officer calling from the police station. Your mother is here and wants to speak with you. This call is also being recorded."

"Okay…"

"Hello, Shikesh, I am at the police station and won't be able to pick up your brother from school, so you can phone your dad and tell him. I will give you the number for the school, so you can tell them."

"Okay, what's the number?" I wrote the number. "Why are you at the police station?"

There were a few seconds of silence. "Don't worry, I can't talk. I have to go now, bye."

"Okay, bye."

I phoned my father twice and there was no answer, so I then phoned the school to inform them that my youngest brother's mother wouldn't be picking him up, so his father would.

After the phone call to the school, I felt like something wasn't right, so I phoned the school again to ask if my youngest brother had received the message.

"Hello, I called earlier and just want to know if my youngest brother got the message?" I asked.

"Um, I told him that his uncle would pick him up, and he ran out of school. I tried to run after him but he ran so fast."

"Okay…" I panicked. "Do you know where he went out of the school?"

"I don't know… I'll check again and call you back."

"Okay, please call me when you know."

My other younger brother arrived home, so I told him what happened. As we had never visited the new school which our youngest brother transferred to, he looked up the directions.

I went back upstairs in case I saw my youngest brother coming home on his own. A minute later, my phone rang.

"Hello, I am the deputy head teacher and have just been told what happened. We don't know where he is and cannot see him anywhere near the school," he said.

"Thank you for calling me back! I just hope that he's okay and nothing has happened… maybe he has made his own way home?"

A few seconds later, my youngest brother was walking towards the house, so I ran downstairs to open the door. As soon as he got in the house, he dropped to his knees and cried while I was still on the phone to the deputy head teacher.

I held him in my arms. "Hey, it's okay... what happened?"

He cried. "I got bullied in my last lesson and then when the teacher told me my uncle was picking me up, I got scared, so I ran. Dad told me to call this boy in a year above me an evil person and his friend pushed me."

The deputy head teacher then said goodbye as I needed to look after my youngest brother. I phoned my father again, and he answered, so I told him what happened and he came home.

Once he got home, I expressed how angry I was and told him how the situation made me feel. The reason why I was so angry is because of what I heard my youngest brother tell me.

A few weeks before this day, my father was speaking to my youngest brother, and he told him to call a boy in his school "an evil person" if he ever came up to my youngest brother. The boy who my father was talking about is the son of my father's eldest brother.

I thought, "Why did my father want my youngest brother to say such a thing and what did he tell him about his eldest brother which scared him so much?"

My father then stood up and walked into another room.

"Do you think you're the only one suffering? Others are suffering too," he said.

I didn't reply because I knew an argument would occur and he would manipulate the truth. Later that evening, my father was speaking to my younger brother while I was upstairs.

"She has been arrested for attacking someone. If they don't do anything, then I will go next!" he said.

I didn't sleep well that night because I was concerned about who my mother had hurt and why? I then thought back to the night before because I had overheard a conversation between my parents.

"Do you want to listen to me?" my father asked my mother.

I didn't hear a reply from my mother, so I am assuming that she nodded her head to say yes or spoke quietly.

"You can do something before me," my father said.

The next morning, I went downstairs to have breakfast and the house phone rang, so I picked it up. It was my mother's solicitor, so I handed the phone to my father.

I felt very vulnerable because I was so tired and didn't sleep well. I couldn't stop thinking about what my mother may have done and to whom? It was around 1:00pm in the afternoon when my parents came home. They were both laughing and so happy about what my mother had done. I was in such disbelief and didn't know what to think? Both of my younger brothers were listening to my father.

"Your mum is a real woman now! Before she didn't do anything and was a coward. Now she isn't!" he said with a raised voice.

I went downstairs with my water bottle to make it look like I went to get water. I wanted to make sure that my mother was at home and I wasn't just imagining it.

The reason why I was so uncertain is because if my father had also done something, then my parents may have gone to prison and my father's plan to give me the responsibility which he always wanted to would have become a reality and that's what I didn't want!

While filling up my water bottle, I overheard a conversation between my parents.

"Look, I will be at work and you can't go near the school because of bail conditions, so we have to use him," my father said.

I was walking out of the kitchen and my mother approached me.

"What do you want to eat son?" she asked in Gujarati with a smile.

"What did you do?"

"You know your father's eldest brother? I hurt him badly," she laughed.

"How did you hurt him?"

"I pushed him from behind and when he turned around, I hit him on his face with scissors."

My younger brother walked into the kitchen and stood in front of me. After a few seconds, my father joined us which made the environment very uncomfortable for me.

"Tell me what you did again?" I asked my mother.

She looked towards my father and didn't know what to say. Why was she looking at my father when he wasn't at the scene? I realised that it was a planned attack and whatever she would say from that moment onwards, it would be what my father would tell her to say.

"Nah, she did what she had to," my father said.

My mother laughed again while saying, "Even if I am found guilty, I won't go to prison and nothing will happen to me."

I looked at my younger brother in disbelief as he reminded me about my father's second eldest brother's death anniversary. From the way my parents looked at me, it was confirmed that my mother attacked my father's eldest brother because they planned it and not because it was self-defense.

My father wanted to mark his brother's death anniversary in his own way because he believed that he was murdered and their eldest brother was involved which was never proven. Whenever he hasn't been able to back up his words, he would say, "The psychic told me, so that's why I believe it."

The way I have been controlled by my father, he would know when I would be vulnerable and this would be the time when he would gain control over me. While standing in the kitchen with my parents, I felt like telling them that I would take the responsibility and before saying anything, I reminded myself that they would only speak nicely if they wanted something from me.

In that moment, I left the kitchen and went to my room where I cried. By overhearing the conversation while getting water, I knew that my parents wanted to use me to pick up and drop my youngest brother to and from school.

They assumed that I wasn't doing anything even though they knew of my plans because before my mother betrayed me, she knew what I would be doing until the end of 2016. She would also tell my father everything that she knew, so he also knew of my plans.

By walking out of the kitchen and not staying there, I saved myself from being controlled by my parents and because of this, I grew the strength in knowing that they would never unconditionally love me because all they saw me as was a resource.

I also realised that if my youngest brother called my father's eldest brother's son "an evil person," then he would tell his father who would then approach my mother and this would give her a chance to hurt him and claim self-defense while making up a false story about him.

This is why my father brainwashed my youngest brother with such fearful lies because my parents could then use his vulnerability to their advantage during the court case. By reminding myself of everything that my father has taught me about committing a crime and making it look like self-defense, I know what the truth really is and that's all that matters.

I woke up the next morning and laid in bed while thinking about whether I would start speaking to my parents again or not? After thinking it all through, I made a decision before going downstairs to have breakfast.

My mother stood up behind me. "Shikesh, I haven't warmed up the milk," she said in Gujarati.

"I'm not speaking to you," I pointed my finger towards her without looking back.

After having breakfast, I went to my room and the vulnerability that I felt before, it completely disappeared because it felt like I broke out of their control for good! During this time, I learnt to let go of things which I couldn't control and to only focus on what I could control. By having my strength back, I was even more determined to launch my business, so I carried on with my business planning.

On Friday 24th June 2016, I woke up early and was so excited about the day because I had planned to work on my website template. I had so many ideas and couldn't wait to start after having breakfast.

I walked into the living room and my parents were sitting on the sofa.

"All right, son?" my father asked.

I ignored him and walked into the kitchen.

"You will have to be in court for two days next week, so we need to sit down and talk. We have to discuss it all and I need to update you on what's been happening because we haven't talked. The solicitor also needs to speak with you. Are you listening?" he said.

"Yes, I heard what you said. Don't worry, I don't need to sit down and talk because I know exactly what I need to say."

"That's good then if you know what to say."

I sat down to have breakfast and my father was still talking. Even after asking him three times in a calm voice to let me eat, he still didn't stop.

"You act like it's always been others who have hurt me and you haven't done anything?" I said.

He raised his voice while giving me evil looks. "I haven't ever hurt you! If I can give my money away, then I can do anything."

I felt so suffocated and when I looked back at my father, his intimidation provoked me, so I slammed my water bottle on the table while holding it in my hand and then stood up before pushing the dining chair down into the kitchen.

"I am going to start a war in this house! You blamed me for my eldest brother failing his university and she blamed me that it's my fault my younger brother lost weight and if he fails his GCSE's, then it will be my fault too? I haven't done anything wrong yet I am being blamed for everything?" I said.

"I will call police and have you arrested," he replied.

"Arrested for what?"

"Shouting."

"Shouting?"

"You are threatening me by shouting."

"How am I threatening you by shouting? I came down to eat, and you began speaking to me. I asked you three times in a calm voice to let me eat and you didn't stop speaking. You intimidated me by giving me evil looks and now I am the one who is threatening you? Do you think that I even care if I get arrested? Call them right now and have me arrested, go on!" He went silent. "You know what, I'll do you a favour, I'll call them for you!"

My parents ran towards me and grabbed my left arm as hard as they could while I was holding my phone in my right hand. As they couldn't reach my phone, I was able to dial 999.

"Hello, which service do you need?" he asked.

"Police please."

My parents let go of my arm and my father went into the bathroom to freshen up while my mother stood in the kitchen facing a picture of God to pray.

While I was on the phone, I told the police officer what had happened and I cannot remember everything because a lot was said. My father then came out of the bathroom and sat on the sofa while putting his shoes on.

"I want you to leave my house. Find a room today," he said with his arms folded.

"Do you think that I'm going to leave that easily?"

After fifteen minutes, the doorbell rang, so I went to answer it. There were about five to six police officers in the house and my father interrupted me every time he thought I would say something to expose the truth. Instead of allowing me to explain how I felt from what he made me experience, he indirectly threatened me by telling me that he would put my belongings outside of the house if I shouted again and he wouldn't even need my permission.

I became silent once the police officer agreed with him and the reason for the argument that day was something that I couldn't remember in that moment. I also couldn't remember the incident which happened on the 31st December 2015 because I went into protection mode and all I could focus on was keeping myself safe.

Now that my father wasn't able to control me, he knew what he needed to do if I was to speak the truth. Becoming homeless was my fear, so he achieved his goal of keeping me silent. Both of my parents portrayed me as someone on benefits, not having a job, causing trouble and being a harm to their younger kids? Everything that they said was a lie!

The police officer told me if I wanted my money back, then I would have to go through the court and when I told him that it wasn't about the money and about something else, I cannot remember what he said. As I was still feeling angry from the intimidation that my father made me experience, the police officer asked me to go for a thirty-minute walk to calm down.

Before going to my room to get changed, I replied to my father about something that he said and the lady police officer who was stood beside me, she told me not to argue in front of her. It made me feel like my parents aim of making me look like the problem was achieved.

When I came back home later that day, I approached my mother, and she was crying a little.

"Call your solicitor and tell him that I want to speak to him," I said.

"I have to ask him first because he doesn't need to talk to you. He hasn't asked for you. Just look after yourself and live your life. You're not well, just look after yourself."

"I am well and there is nothing wrong with me! Why do you keep telling me that I am not well when there is nothing wrong with me?"

"Just live your life."

I went to my room and reflected on why my father would lie and make me believe that my mother's solicitor wanted to speak with me when he didn't need to? Why did he tell me that I needed to be in court when I didn't need to be?

After going over everything that was said, my father's intentions were exposed. He wanted to use me to testify in court on behalf of my mother and the reason why he wanted to speak to me was to make sure that I would say what he wanted me to say.

From the response that I gave, he understood that he couldn't use me any longer, so I became a threat to his plan and because of this, his goal was now to do whatever he could to either make me homeless or send me to prison for attacking him.

If he was to achieve this, then every lie which he told the police about me would have become a reality and no one would have believed a word that I would have said. This is what my father wanted when he realised that I had broken out of his control.

The intimidation and provocation that he made me experience for the next few weeks, it made me realise how desperate he was. What kept me calm was the fear of becoming homeless and as I became physically sick and severely suicidal, I stopped eating and looking after myself.

In the evening that same day, I overheard a conversation between my parents.

"Why did you blame him about his younger brother?" my father asked my mother.

"Look, he was talking with loud voice and I didn't know what to say."

"Look, I don't care about you and I don't care about him!"

There were a few seconds of silence.

"If he shouts again, we can put his things outside and we don't even need to tell him. Why should we suffer?" my father said.

I got in touch with the same housing officer as I did in January 2016 and he couldn't help me as much because he had another job. What I couldn't understand is how I still felt that I needed to stay at home and not leave? Why did I feel more vulnerable with the thought of leaving when I should have felt happy to leave?

It seems like subconsciously, the commitment that I made to myself on Monday 28th November 2011 about finding the truth, it kept me going no matter how vulnerable I was.

After two weeks of living in such fear, I gained the strength to become emotionally resilient which helped me to carry on with my business planning.

I thought, "If something will happen, then let it because I can't keep living with the fear of going out and coming back to find my things outside. If this is what will happen, then let it and if it does, I will deal with it! I need to carry on with my life because if I can overcome everything that I have and achieve so many things until today, then I can do it again!"

The energy that I felt after having this thought scared me because the motivation which I now had, it would allow me to achieve something which would destroy every threat and vulnerability that my father had made me experience since my childhood.

On Monday 27th June 2016, I received a phone call from the police officer who was in charge of my abuse case. She informed me that nothing would happen due to lack of evidence and as my parents didn't give a statement, nothing more could be done.

Even though a small part of me wanted the case to go to court, I knew what the outcome would be. I also knew that my eldest brother was prepared on what to say and how to say it because my father had informed him about it after both of my parents were interviewed. My father had also emailed my eldest brother, and I knew this from overhearing a conversation.

When she told me that she believed me, I felt peace and could also hear the frustration in her voice of not being able to do more. Thank you so much for all of the support and believing in me!

I cannot remember how long it was after this day when I received another phone call from another police officer who wanted to talk about the incident on the 24th June 2016. When I called the police on the day, I felt more helpless after they left, so to receive a follow-up phone call, it made me feel less traumatised because the conversation was very reassuring.

Thank you for calling me and helping me understand that my voice was heard and not ignored.

My full commitment to launching my business felt more certain because on Friday 22nd July 2016, I ordered most of the business equipment and stationery that I needed to become self-employed as a Personal Life Coach. Everything else that I needed was ordered at a later date.

I have never unboxed so many things in my entire life in one day! It felt like Christmas had come early and even though it was only business equipment and stationery; it was still so exciting because I would achieve something huge when just a few weeks ago; I was suicidal for the sixth time!

It was during mid-August 2016 when my younger brother came home with his GCSE results. As soon as he opened the front door, my heart dropped, and all I wanted to do was break down and cry because for so many weeks, I was living with the belief that it would have been my fault if he had failed his GCSE's. My mother's words left a deep scare within me until that day.

My younger brother went into the room that my parents were in. "I passed!" he said.

The feeling that I experienced when I heard those words is something that I can't explain. My mother hurt me so much and I don't know how I would have dealt with a situation of my younger brother failing. It just shows how much words can hurt you.

My grandmother's death anniversary was coming up and I could feel some strong energy in the air. It was a very uncertain moment, and I kept feeling very uncomfortable with the thought of not being happy if I didn't prove my innocence.

Even though the thought of starting my business always excited me, having to live with my parents getting away with everything that they made me experience was a thought which broke me a little each day.

Monday 8th August 2016 had now arrived, and I kept thinking about my parents diaries. I was so eager to have something which would prove they were guilty and during a call to God for his guidance; I found myself in complete silence.

Thirty minutes later, I watched a film called "The Lovely Bones." I believe that no matter what we watch, listen to, who we talk to, and so on, it always happens in the right moment when it's meant to.

Towards the end of the film, there was a part where a diary was found which had the truth and once the film was over, I thanked God for showing me what I needed to do!

I woke up early on Sunday 14th August 2016 and realised that my parents and younger brothers were going to the Temple and would be there the whole day as it was a Hindu festival. I freshened up and without having any breakfast or lunch; I went through my parents diaries to see what I could find?

My focus was now back on launching my business and I was setting everything up. I designed the templates, ordered business cards and did everything that I needed to do.

As I was still on benefits, I had to let DWP – Department for Work and Pensions know that I would be doing permitted work, so I needed to make sure that the form was sent to them on time.

I realised that it would take two weeks for the form to be processed and this is where I panicked because I didn't realise this before. The form played a very important part because if it was rejected, then I wouldn't have been able to launch my business.

After putting in so much work, it would have left me feeling like a failure if the form wasn't accepted because everything was prepared and ready to go!

It was Tuesday 20th September 2016 and I couldn't handle the wait any longer because I needed to know if the form was accepted, so I phoned DWP about it.

My heart raced, and I panicked as I was in the waiting line. I couldn't stop thinking about how hard I had worked and had everything prepared in just two months! The thought of being told that the form wasn't accepted would have made me take the wrong turn in life until I thought, "If they reject my form, then I will work over sixteen hours a week and sign off benefits, so either way, I will launch my business!

I now felt peace because I had a solution and all of the hard work that I had put in, it wouldn't have gone to waste.

"Hello, may I take your name please?" he asked.

"Hello, it's Mr. Shikesh Sorathia."

"And your National Insurance number?" I gave him my details to pass security.

"Thank you. How may I help you today?"

"I am calling about permitted work. I sent in the form two weeks ago and phoned in last week to confirm if DWP had received it. I was told that I would get a phone call to tell me about the decision by the end of the week. I haven't received a phone call, so I would like to know what the outcome was?"

"Okay, let me just check for you. It says the meeting was held yesterday and everything seems okay."

"Does that mean that the form was accepted and I can start self-employment as permitted work?"

"Yes. Everything is fine here, so you can."

My eyes lit up. "That's great news! Thank you so much! Is there anything else that I need to do or send you any documents?"

"You're welcome. No, you don't need to send anything. Is there anything else I can do for you today?"

"No, there isn't. You have helped me with my enquiry, thank you so much again!"

"Okay, take care then."

"Thank you, take care and have a great rest of the week, bye."

"Thank you and you too, bye."

"Bye."

Thursday 22nd September 2016 was now in town and I turned twenty-five years of age. It wasn't just my birthday; it was also the day of my business launch!

After experiencing so many difficulties throughout the year, I wasn't going to let my parents take me off track no matter what they may have said or done! Once I had breakfast, I got on with the day. There was one more thing which I needed to do to make my business official and that was to sign up with HMRC – Her Majesty's Revenue and Customs. This would allow me to pay my business taxes and National Insurance each year.

Choosing my birthday to launch my business was a way to reclaim myself in every way and to not dislike any part of me. I have learnt that no matter how happy you might be, if you dislike even the smallest part of yourself, then it can leave you feeling lost.

It was so essential for me to reclaim myself because the time had arrived for me to break away from my past which would allow me to become the person that I had always desired to be!

Starting my Life Coaching Diploma on my birthday was just the fuel which was added. Launching my business on my birthday was the oxygen and match which gave power to my flame that can never be put out ever again!

After completing the day, I sat in my room for a few minutes to take it all in. I couldn't believe what I had achieved and after so many years of feeling broken, I felt a spiritual rebirth once again.

As I had ordered grocery shopping to enjoy on the day, I made my way downstairs to have a feast! I walked out of my room and could hear my mother in the kitchen cooking and from the smell; I knew that she was cooking Indian food which she would only cook during festival times.

"Happy Birthday," she said.

I ignored her and sat down on the sofa next to my younger brother while thinking, "If she thinks that her food will make me forget how she abused me throughout the year, then she is wrong because nothing will ever make me forget how she treated me!"

My mother's presence in the kitchen made me feel suffocated, so I reassured myself by knowing that what I was feeling, it wouldn't last.

"Happy Birthday," my younger brother said.

"Thank you."

Once my youngest brother was home from school, he wished me a Happy Birthday also. My father said nothing and from the silence between my parents that evening, I knew that they felt so much guilt for how they had treated me over the years.

The evening had now arrived and after having dinner, it was time to light up the sky with my younger brothers. Before doing any fireworks, I looked up at the sky and saw a single twinkling star which made me feel warmth inside of my heart.

I smiled while thinking, "That star is for me tonight."

There were seven rockets remaining when a neighbour approached me from the back road.

"Can you stop it, please? I have to wake up at 5:00am for work tomorrow," he said.

I felt so hurt. "Okay... I'll stop them."

"Please. Stop it, okay?"

"Okay, I will stop now."

The way he approached me and the way that he spoke without even asking why I was doing fireworks, it hurt me a lot! I felt so hurt where I couldn't even explain why I was doing them. The remaining rockets were sent into the sky the following evening.

To make my birthday more special, a friend treated me to a day out in the city where every moment was amazing and emotional at the same time as we reflected on how far I had come. Thank you so much for the birthday treat my friend! I enjoyed every single moment and always think about it.

It was the end of 2016 and even though it was a very painful year to begin with; it wasn't all bad towards the end. Before the year ended, I was sitting downstairs with both of my younger brothers while our mother was in the kitchen.

"You know, I haven't taken a bath for a month," my youngest brother said.

I looked at my other younger brother before looking back at my youngest brother. "What did you say?"

"I haven't taken a bath for a month."

"Why? Please get a new pair of clothes and towel from your wardrobe and have a bath this minute."

I was showing him how to operate the shower when my mother walked into the bathroom.

"Do you want me to help you have a bath?" she asked my youngest brother.

"No, it's okay."

"If you need help then call me, okay?" she said.

"Okay."

I couldn't understand why he hadn't taken a bath for a month? I thought, "Are my parents focused on their own agenda so much where they haven't even cared about their own son's well-being?"

On New Year's Eve, I reflected over the whole year and thought about what I wanted to leave behind and take with me into the New Year. There were a lot of negative emotions, feelings and thoughts which I needed to destroy and by moving on from them, I could allow new emotions, feelings and thoughts to enter my life by experiencing new positive events.

Entering 2017 wasn't as bad as how 2016 began because everything was going well and I was getting to know my business better.

Becoming self-employed isn't an easy journey because there will be many moments where you think about giving up. Even though it will seem impossible at first, if you truly believe in your vision and you know that you can follow through with your mission, then nothing will stop you from building your empire.

I was looking forward to what the year would bring until lightning struck! It was Saturday 1st April 2017, and I heard my parents talking while I was having breakfast. My younger brothers were sitting with them.

"He was questioned yesterday last year wasn't he?" my father asked.

"Today is 1st April," my mother replied.

My father became shocked. "Today is 1st April? I thought yesterday was 1st April. That's why I brought pizza and we ate it."

After having breakfast, I went to my room and felt uncomfortable. I felt anger and frustration because I couldn't understand why I was having to experience such abuse? Having to live in such an environment where you're being reminded about what you experienced as a child is worse than thinking about suicide.

It was 2:00pm that same day and I didn't want to wait any longer to eat lunch. I could hear my mother cooking and from the smell, I could tell that it was food that she would only cook during festivals.

From the conversation which I overheard in the morning, I knew what my parents' intentions were. I thought, "I won't eat today because I don't want them to make things harder for me by being downstairs… why do I have to think like this when I haven't done anything wrong and all I want to do is eat?"

I decided to go downstairs to eat lunch and as I couldn't hear my father's voice, I assumed that he wasn't sitting in the living room. When I opened the living room door, my father was sitting on the sofa with his phone in his hand while continuously giving me an evil look. I looked back at him before walking into the kitchen.

My father stayed in another room since 2016 when I would be downstairs, so this made me realise how I wasn't mistaken in knowing that he had an evil agenda that day.

In the past when we were speaking, he would say something like, "I don't like looking at your face because it reminds me of how you're living and I don't like to think about it. When the time will come, I will take my anger out on this paedophile ring because they are to blame for how your life is."

Once I was in the kitchen, I started making a sandwich and the way my father looked at me, it made me feel suffocated like I couldn't breathe. It felt like I needed to run yet I couldn't?

"Do you think that you've won?" I said to my mother quietly. "You haven't won and you will never win! All three of you will go to prison and do you think that I won't make it happen? Do you think that you are something big by cooking this food? I know why you're cooking this food!"

My younger brother then told my father that I was arguing with my mother and in a quiet voice, he was telling me to keep quiet while swearing at me.

I walked into the living room and looked at my younger brother.

"She blamed me for your weight loss and told me that if you failed your GCSE's, then it would have been my fault. You don't know how they've been treating me!"

"I said those words because I was depressed! I didn't mean to say those words!" my mother said.

"If you don't leave my house, I will give you notice to quit," my father said.

"Why should I leave just because you're telling me to go?"

He pointed at my younger brothers. "Because you're speaking in front of my two kids."

"You speak to them all the time and tell them so many things but when I talk about things so they know who their parents are, it's a crime to you?"

"You better leave my house soon!"

"I've been wanting to leave since 2010 voluntarily but I couldn't because of what you've been telling me! You've been emotionally abusing me since 2010 and taking my money where you haven't paid a penny back! It's because of you I'm in this position, so do you think that I will leave just because you're telling me to go?"

"Just shut the…"

"I will take you, your wife and your eldest son to court if you want me to leave. That's the only way I will leave if you want me to go right now! I promise you, I have evidence to prove all three of you are guilty!"

Everything that I said was being twisted, and it made me realise how much they had improved in making themselves look innocent because everything that they said to me, it would have made the police believe them. The thought of taking them to court became uncertain as I knew that they would humiliate me, destroy me and then get away with years of abuse.

My mother started crying, so my youngest brother went upstairs. My father started swearing at me like he always did as I was apologising to my youngest brother for what he was having to experience. He wasn't upset with me or anything and I could tell that he understood why I was so angry.

"If your eldest son didn't confess in front of you that he abused me, then swear on your father in front of my younger brother!" I said to my father.

"No, I won't."

"If you were telling the truth, then you wouldn't have a problem with it. The only reason why someone wouldn't swear on their father is because they are guilty."

"No, I won't swear on my father. I will only swear on my ancestors."

"Why on your ancestors and not your father?"

"Because I don't want to."

"If you can swear on your ancestors, then you can swear on your father!"

"No, I won't swear on my father," he showed an evil smirk before looking at my younger brother. "Did I start anything today?"

My younger brother nodded. "No."

I looked at my father. "I started it because you told her to cook this food! You're celebrating that your son got away with sexual abuse charges! I know he was questioned today last year!"

"I am making this food for your youngest brother! He said he wanted to eat!" my mother said.

"The reason why you made this food is because you're celebrating the victory you feel, so you can say whatever you want because deep down you know I'm right!"

There was silence.

"You better leave my house or I will give you notice to quit," my father said.

"Do you think that I care if you give me notice to quit? Before you even get a chance to give it to me, you will be arrested and harassment won't be the only charges! I promise you, I have evidence to prove you are guilty! I have bank statements which show every transaction going to you when you were emotionally abusing me!"

"Show them to me?" my father asked.

"No, I will show you in court!"

I looked at my younger brother. "I want to know something and please, tell me the truth. Am I any harm to you… have I ever been any threat to you?"

"If you take them to court and our youngest brother goes into care because of it and I won't be able to look after him, then yes, you are harm to me, otherwise, you are no harm to me."

"That's all I wanted to know because I know that I have never been any harm to you both. That's what he said in front of the police last year when I called them. He said that I am harm to you both."

There was silence.

"You have done evil thing to this family," my father said.

"What evil thing? You have been telling me since 2010 that I have done an evil thing to this family and whenever I ask for an explanation, you tell me the same story but never a direct answer to what I have done? The reason why you don't have an answer is because I haven't done any evil thing!"

I looked at my mother. "I had to ask you five times last year if I did anything wrong to this family and you said no with a raised voice and an evil look. That's how much guilt you have been carrying! You're not going to say anything now, no? Before you couldn't shut your mouth because you felt that I couldn't say anything and now you're staying quiet because you know he's guilty!"

"You have done evil to this family," my father said again.

"If anyone has done an evil thing to this family, then it's you, your wife and your eldest son! You have taken advantage of me in every way and haven't even been grateful for how much I have done.

Because of me, your mother had a funeral, you still have a roof over your head, there were fireworks during festival times. Your eldest son also benefited with money from me when he was lying behind my back! He had two new suits to wear to work at his new job on his first day!"

"You spent the money on fireworks because you wanted to!" my mother said.

"I spent the money on fireworks so my younger brothers didn't feel left out and you enjoyed it also, so why are you being so ungrateful?"

"You didn't have to spend that much on fireworks. Why did you?" my father asked.

"We used to do fireworks on five days throughout the year. The amount that I spent, it wasn't that much at all!" I looked at my mother. "You begged for my help and wanted me to speak for you at the end of 2015. After I was there for you, you decided to betray me and I know it's because he told you to! Nothing has ever happened without him being involved!"

"Why couldn't you speak about the abuse when you were little?" my father asked.

"You keep asking me the same question and I have given you the same answer so many times! You used to beat her so badly, and I was always afraid of you!"

My father had an evil smirk on his face.

"He has only slapped me twice in my life!" my mother said.

"Are you serious? You want to lie to me when I have seen it myself? He has done more than just slap you!"

"He is my husband! If I do something wrong, then he has a right to hit me!"

"Are you serious?" I was in such disbelief. "So many females are dying every day because of domestic violence and you think that it's okay to say such a thing to me? So much work goes into helping people who have suffered with domestic violence and you want to sit there and tell me that it's okay?"

"Are you saying she can't be depressed?" my father asked.

"I am not saying that at all!"

I looked at my mother. "Do you know what they do to people in prison who support child abuse?"

"Whatever happens, God Krishna is there for me and he will look after me," she replied while crying.

"I don't care about your tears because you never cared about mine. Cry as much as you like because it won't save you! You're crying because you know that you're guilty and you're scared about what will happen! It seems like every time I mention your eldest son, you start crying but when I talk about myself, you never cry?"

"I'm crying because of both of you! Both of my sons life is taken away."

"Your husband has hurt me and that's why my life has been taken away. He's the reason for me being in this position and after everything that I did for you, you betrayed me, so you are to blame also!"

I looked at my father. "I hope you die in prison!"

"If you die before me, I won't give you a funeral," he replied.

"You won't give me a funeral?"

"No, I won't."

"Do you think that I even want you to give me a funeral after everything that you have put me through? If I die before you, my body won't even be coming to this house! After how much pain you have caused me, you will never be allowed to say goodbye to me!"

My father held a TV remote and pointed it at me.

"Put it down! Put it down now!" I commanded.

"I am not doing anything."

"Pointing it at me can be seen as a threat!"

"No, it's not a threat."

"Yes, it is!" I looked at my younger brother. "It can be seen as a threat, can't it?"

He put his hand our father's shoulder as he nodded. "Dad, put it down," he said.

"I am not doing anything, I am just holding it. Look, I am just holding it."

"If I was to hit you right now, then it would be self-defense. You already know that though because you know the law better than anyone else," I replied.

I looked at my younger brother. "Do you remember at the end of December 2015 when he showed us the copper pipe with the knife stuck into one end of it?"

My father looked at him. "You don't remember, yeah?" he said with anger in his voice.

My younger brother panicked. "Yeah, no, I don't remember," he then looked away from me.

I looked at my father. "Do you really think that I don't know what's going on? I am sitting right here and you're telling him to lie?"

"You're mentally ill, it's all in your head," my father said as I cried.

"Look, look what he's doing. We haven't done anything to him!" my father said to my mother.

It felt like I couldn't breathe and I found it hard to speak.

"I forgive you! I forgive all three of you and I am sorry if I ever hurt any of you without knowing!" I said while crying

"You don't have to say sorry to anyone," my parents replied.

"I do, because you keep telling me that I have done such an evil thing to this family! Let me make it clear though, I am not forgiving you for what you did to me because it will never be okay! I am forgiving you because I need to let go of this anger now, otherwise, I will turn mentally ill!"

"I will admit one thing, I shouldn't have taken your money," my father said with guilt showing in his eyes.

I stood up to get water because I still couldn't breathe. It felt like I was having a panic attack and wasn't sure what to do. I sat down again and did breathing exercises.

"I don't want to make this food but I have to. I don't feel like making this food but I have no choice," my mother said while my father was in the bathroom.

If my youngest brother wanted to eat the food, and he told my mother to make it, then she wouldn't have said such a thing as she would have been happy to make it. I also realised that she only said it because of the guilt that she felt and that's why when my father was in the bathroom, she indirectly admitted that I was right for why she was making the food.

When my father had slipped up on his words when I asked him certain questions, he told me that I was putting words in his mouth to stay away from admitting the truth and before I told my parents that I forgave them, my father said, "You have emotionally abused me too. If you are saying I have done all of that to you, then I did it because you made me do it."

When I think about victim blaming, it's a way for the guilty to say that they are guilty without directly saying it.

This argument went on for five hours and before I went to my room to sleep, I apologised to both of my younger brothers. They were very understanding and knew why I was feeling so upset. I also told my parents that I would leave whenever my time had arrived and once I was gone, they would never see me again.

Once I was in my room, I heard my father tell my younger brother, "If he was really brave, he would have gone to the police station to report the abuse, isn't it?"

The next morning, I woke up feeling so positive and instantly knew why I didn't feel broken. The commitment that I made to myself on Monday 28th November 2011 of wanting to know why I had suffered so many years of abuse, it was achieved!

I believe the argument needed to happen because I couldn't have stopped it no matter what I may have done. It was time for me to know the truth and even though it was painful to hear what my parents told me during the argument; it brought me closure because my search in knowing why I suffered for twenty years was over.

Two months before this argument, I was sitting on my bed before starting work and I became very emotional. After a few minutes, I cried while saying, "God, please help me to let go of the past. I am giving all of my worries and problems to you because I don't know how to deal with them anymore."

During this moment, I felt a warmth in my heart and I couldn't understand why I felt so strongly about forgiving everyone who had hurt me? While still crying, I said, "I forgive you three for what you have done to me. I forgive you today and I am letting go of the anger because I need to move on with my life now. I am also forgiving everyone else who hurt me in my past."

It seemed like forgiving my parents and eldest brother on my own wasn't enough as I forgave them during the argument also. The night before I forgave them on my own, I felt so strongly about never forgiving them for what they had made me experience. Once I experienced it, I was shocked! From this day, I learnt to not force things to happen because if something is meant to happen, then it will happen so naturally when you least expect it.

I never understood what forgiveness meant until I experienced it because I assumed that you would be saying what happened to you, it was okay? The real meaning of forgiveness is to let go of the anger, so you don't keep hurting yourself and by doing this, you're allowing yourself to be free forever. Forgiveness will never be about saying what happened was okay! It will always be about you and your happiness only and not about the people who have hurt you.

When I researched about it to gain a better understanding, I learnt that not everyone needs to forgive the people who hurt them because they can feel free without experiencing it. If you cannot move on from the pain which you might be experiencing from what people have made you experience, then forgiveness can be a way for you to let go of the pain so you can be free and happy.

My life was about to become even more worthwhile! I received a message from a friend in the morning of Friday 5th May 2017 and there was a link to a website. While reading through it, I was uncertain about attending the event because I had come across so many similar events in the past and felt that they weren't for me.

I signed up to it in the end as I thought, "What will I lose?" I had never heard of Andy Harrington before that day, so I researched about him which helped me to understand how he became so successful. The event which I signed up to was his live event called Power To Achieve.

As the event was a few weeks away, I worked through his audio programme and reflected on what I could achieve and whether I would even develop as a person?

By attending the event, I had no energy left when I got home on the final day! The event team had recommended to stay in a hotel close to the venue yet I traveled on all three days instead.

I thought, "I need to show myself that I will do whatever it takes to achieve my dreams and not hurt anyone along the way, so I will travel to and from the event on all three days because this is how committed I need to be!"

I left my house before 5am on Friday and Saturday as I wanted to make sure that I was always on time. Whenever I have had to be somewhere, I have always been at least thirty minutes early because you never know what may happen during your journey. Even though

I would be thirty minutes early, for me, it's all about the peace of mind where you're not rushing around trying to get somewhere.

On the last day of the event, I left my house before 6am as the public transport has different times for Sunday. Apart from Sunday when I came home by 8pm, I arrived home after 11pm on Friday and Saturday.

The question which I had before attending the event, "What will I lose?" I lost nothing because the amount that I gained, it wasn't known right away until I reflected on the event after a few days and what I experienced at the event itself is a whole different story!

Sometimes in life, we will say no to something and then later on, we won't even think about it and just do it. This is what I mean by something happening so naturally because when it's meant to happen, it really will.

I want to thank my friend for sending me the link to the event because I wouldn't have achieved how much I did otherwise. I also want to thank Andy Harrington for speaking to me on the last day and hugging me twice. Before going home, I knew that I had to thank you personally because your event was so powerful and the way you saw me cry when we spoke, it wasn't planned!

Lastly, I want to thank everyone who I met at the event for supporting me and getting me through all three days.

It was the end of August 2017 when my younger brother knocked on my door.

"One minute," I said before opening the door.

"Dad said you need to move into the next room because we're getting lodgers for extra money."

"Okay, I'll just move in now as I've just finished work."

I began moving my things into the next room when I realised that my privacy would be taken away from me and with little space, I wouldn't have been able to work.

"I'm moving my things back in the room that I was in," I said to my younger brother.

"Why?"

"I am registered with data protection, so I have to keep everything locked and the way I will work, it will not be easy. Our parents will also want the CCTV on, so they will tell me to leave the room unlocked. I can't do that because my work is more important than their own agenda."

A day or two later, I was about to have lunch when my younger brother approached me.

"You have to move into the other room because the mortgage company are taking us to court, so we need the room for lodgers," he said.

"I already told you why I can't do that and it's not that I am stopping them to get lodgers."

"The CCTV will be off."

"That's what they have said in the past and then harassed me because they wanted it on. I am not going to work like that! If they are saying that the CCTV will remain off, then what problem do they have with putting lodgers in that room, you tell me that?"

He remained silent.

After over hearing a conversation, I became aware that my mother's court case had a final hearing on Tuesday 5th September 2017 where she would either be found guilty or not guilty. I also knew that my father had to go to court for another reason and I wasn't sure why even though I thought that it could be about the mortgage?

Tuesday 5th September 2017 arrived, and I decided not to do much work because I was distracted by knowing that it was my mother's final hearing. I wished that my mother wouldn't win because I knew she was guilty and if she was to get away with it, then I wouldn't be able to trust myself in reporting anything to the police ever again unless I had no other option.

I also thought, "If she gets away with it, then I can prove what needs to be improved within the justice system because I wasn't interviewed by anyone during the whole investigation and when my mother was talking about issues from past years, then surely the court would have wanted to speak with me?

My parents came home in the evening and my father would normally walk into his room yet he knelt and stroked the cat for a few seconds before standing up and giving me an evil look. A few days after the cat was locked in the neighbours garage, she didn't come back home as she was really traumatised, so my father got a similar cat as my youngest brother was really upset.

Even though I didn't know what the outcome was of my mother's case, I had a slight feeling that she got away with what she had done because if she was found guilty, then she wouldn't have come home.

On Wednesday 13th September 2017, my younger brother knocked on my door.

"Yeah?" I asked.

"I need to talk to you about something important."

"Okay, hold on." I opened the door. "What is it?"

He handed me an envelope. "Because they didn't keep up with the mortgage, dad had to go to court and if he doesn't come up with the money, the house will be repossessed, so you can look for your own place."

I panicked. "What? Where will I go?"

There were papers in the envelope, so I read through them. I cannot remember what I said because I was so furious by reading a letter that was signed by both of my parents where they wrote that they had "borrowed" money from me and once the house was repossessed and before my parents received the remaining amount after their debts were paid off, the mortgage company would have to pay me thirty thousand pounds which was the amount with interest that my parents owed me?

It also stated that it was a "legal document" and it was an agreement between me and my parents?

I thought, "How is this a legal document when it isn't signed by a solicitor or lawyer? It's signed by the people who have made me suffer for twenty years!"

They never paid a penny back and didn't even tell me how much they would pay me, so everything that the letter said was a lie! I read through the letter twice and all I felt was abuse. I almost took my life because of the way my father took money from me and my mother stayed silent while it was all happening. It seemed like my parents thought that they could get away with what they did by manipulating what happened through a letter?

I had planned to come off benefits a week later, so I could start full time self-employment and now my plans were pushed back where I had no control over what was happening.

"There is a second option but dad said he will tell you himself," my younger brother said.

"Did he tell you what it is?"

"No, he said he will tell you himself."

"If I speak to him when he gets home, an argument will occur, so text him right now and ask him because I want to know."

When I read over all of the text messages that were sent between my father and younger brother, I felt suffocated in the same way that I used to feel when he was emotionally abusing me for money. The way he had written his messages was how he used to control me.

My father said that the lender told him to sign a "lodger contract" with me and I would have to make up for his shortfalls? When I asked for this in writing, he said that he made a mistake because the judge told him and not the lender.

I still asked for a written confirmation and when he realised that he got caught lying, he admitted that no one told him because he wanted money from me and that's why he made up two different stories.

My father was also saying that he would sell the house by December 2017 and I could live with them. I felt too broken to understand my father's intentions. I thought, "I can live with them and when I am ready to get a place of my own, then I can move out." This is what my father wanted, and I didn't understand why until later.

That same evening, my younger brother knocked on my door and handed me a letter which my father wrote that evening. It explained how much he wanted from me and I soon realised that he told the lender how he was going sign a "lodger contract" with me where I would pay him his shortfalls. This is how manipulative and abusive he has been towards me.

I woke up the next morning and was thinking about what I could do. After everything that I had experienced until that day, I felt peace while thinking, "I'll give him the amount which he is asking for because if it will stop the house from being repossessed, then my younger brothers and myself won't struggle in the way that we would if we became homeless."

I cried and sat on my bed feeling so helpless because I couldn't understand why I had to rescue my parents after everything that they made me experience? After calming myself down, I thought, "I'll pay the whole debt off, so they don't have to worry about the mortgage at all! The arrears are ten thousand, five hundred and twenty pounds and ninety-seven pence. I have this much, so I'll pay off the mortgage!"

Why was it me who had to save the house after everything that I had experienced? I had already done more than enough for the whole family, so why was it me who had to come to the rescue?

I went downstairs and told my mother to phone my father and tell him that I would pay the whole mortgage off. Once she had spoken to him, she told me that he only wanted one thousand, one hundred, and twenty pounds and not the whole arrears. She also told me that I would get my money back which I didn't believe.

As I hadn't slept or eaten much for two days, I was very vulnerable and if my parents had controlled me like they did in the past, then I wouldn't have been able to stop them because I wasn't able to control my emotions, feelings or thoughts.

The same evening, my father spoke like nothing had happened between us and he tried to shake my hand twice. I reminded myself of 2011 when he shook my hand and still abused me and as I was still aware of how he didn't care about me, I didn't shake his hand.

He told me the same stories as he used to and then told me about my mother's case. I couldn't understand how my mother was found not guilty, and he then mentioned something about a CCTV tape where it would have cost him fifteen thousands pounds and as the barrister and solicitor helped him with it for free, he didn't have to pay that amount?

I thought, "Why would they do it for free and what CCTV tape? My mother told me a different story to what she told the court, so how were my parents able to get away with what they had planned?"

When my father explained that my mother would have spent seven years in prison if she was found guilty, I couldn't understand why he told her that nothing would happen even if she was found guilty? He also told me about the incident on 24th June 2016 when I called the police.

"Social services phoned me after that day and asked about what you had said. I told them you were disturbed about your younger brother being unwell so that's why you were arguing."

If social services phoned my father and wanted to know why I was arguing with him that day, then why didn't they speak to me directly?

Two or three hours went by and he still didn't get to the main motive of the conversation which was about the money to remove the repossession order. After I re-directed the conversation, he showed me a letter which stated what he needed to pay the lender each month.

The amount that he asked for, "one thousand, one hundred and twenty pounds" was the amount my parents needed to pay the lender each month. This confirmed that he was lying and had made up a whole story just to get money from me.

Even when I told him that I would pay the whole mortgage off, he didn't like it because he felt that the lender shouldn't have been paid more than what they were asking for? I couldn't understand why he didn't accept it? He wouldn't have had a mortgage to worry about, so why didn't he accept it? Did he have another agenda?

I felt used because my mother didn't even sit in the same room when I was speaking to my father. I thought, "Her own son is saving her from being homeless and she doesn't even want to show her appreciation? It seems like as long as she will have a roof over her head, she doesn't care about how she treats me?"

I also couldn't believe what she told me earlier that day.

"The judge, jury and all the barristers said they were very proud of me. Your father's eldest brother was told he is a bully, a bad person and his name has been ruined. Your grandfather's and grandmother's name has been made clear they were very good people and can never be put down again."

On the evening of Friday 15th September 2017, my father asked to speak with me and he told me the same stories as he did the night before. He also told me that he couldn't understand why I hated him because he did nothing wrong to me?

I was still very vulnerable and wasn't in the mood for arguing, so I didn't reply.

He held a paper to show me. "This is the postcode which we will move to, so you can look up houses in your spare time."

"I won't be moving with you. Once the house is sold, I will find a place of my own and you will never see me again. I already told you this before and I said it for a reason."

"What if something happens to your mum?"

"I'll be leaving and you will never see me again."

I realised that my father was still planning to go to prison and the only reason why he wanted me to move with them is because he would have told my mother to hurt someone else.

With both of my parents in prison, no one would be there to look after my younger brothers. By realising that my father still wanted to give me the responsibility as he thought that he could try to control me one more time, I got up and went to my room because even though I was so vulnerable, I still had control over my own decisions.

Before I paid the money to my father, he said something like, "I thought I would go to prison and then you all could move but I was wrong because you still would have lost the house. I focused more on going after these people and that's why this situation came because I didn't concentrate on paying the bills."

My father tried to make conversation with me the following evening and as I knew that he only wanted to use me, I cut the conversation short by telling him that once he had paid the lender the money the following Monday, he should tell my younger brother, so I would know. I didn't even look at him. Two days had gone by and he didn't pay the money to the lender which was something that I couldn't understand?

On Monday 18th September 2017, I asked my younger brother if the money was paid? He confirmed that it was and the repossession order was removed.

If my father had been told on the 5th September 2017 of his house being repossessed if he didn't come up with the money, then why was I informed a week later?

I believe it's because my father was thinking of a way to control me and by giving me less time to look for a place of my own, he could play his mind games to get me to do what he wanted. What he didn't realise is that I could never be controlled by him that easily ever again!

For the next few days, I felt so broken and just wanted to crawl into a corner and never come out again. I didn't know why I had to experience such an event and why were my plans pushed back?

Friday 22nd September 2017 had now arrived, and I turned twenty-six years of age. It was also a year's anniversary for my business. By attending the Power To Achieve live event, I was empowered to create new services for my business, so I uploaded my signature coaching programme and Life Coaching Model on my website.

I didn't want anymore pain and the environment at home didn't allow me to breathe. I had so much planned for my life and business and because of my father's evil agenda; I had to put a hold on my plans.

Even though it was a painful month, a friend of mine treated me for my birthday and business anniversary, so it wasn't all bad. Thank you so much for always being there and looking out for me! If it wasn't for you, then I may not have been alive right now.

Before I left home to meet up with my friend for my birthday, I realised that my youngest brother would have been alone at home if I wasn't there. My parents have treated me in this way at least two times where I wouldn't be told anything because they would assume that I would be at home?

It was good to know that my mother would arrive home in thirty minutes, otherwise, I may have had to cancel my plans with my friend. This is another way how my parents haven't care about my life as long as their own agenda has been taken care of.

On Wednesday 27th September 2017, my younger brother knocked on my door.

"Yeah?" I asked.

"I need to talk to you about the front and back garden."

"Okay, one moment." I opened my door. "What about the front and back garden?"

"Dad said if you want, give him money, so he can do the front and back garden. He said you were right, so he wants you to do this."

Before I paid my father the money on 14th September 2017, I told him, "If I pay off the mortgage, then the money that you earn from your work, it can be used to do up the front and back garden because you're saying that you will sell the house by December 2017."

When my father began emotionally abusing me in 2010, he took small amounts of money and then the amount would get larger, so this is what he tried to do again.

I almost called the police because I was so furious and couldn't take anymore abuse from my father. After calming myself down, I wrote a two-page letter expressing how he had made me feel.

Everything that I wrote in the letter would have been what I would have told him on his face and as I knew that I would have beaten him and not stop if I was to speak to him, writing a letter was a safer option for me.

Did my father really think that he could use me again and nothing would happen? I was twenty-six years of age, I was still on benefits and my goal to start full time self-employment didn't happen because of the circumstances that my father brought on me.

I couldn't come off benefits at the time because if I had to live in a place of my own, then I would have had some sort of income at least to help me pay the bills. Even though I had been self-employed for a year, I made no income because I wasn't able to concentrate on work from how my parents were treating me.

My father knew my circumstances, and he felt that his agenda was more important? This is what he did in 2011 where he left me without a penny and it seemed like he wanted to do it again? He knew that I had my own expenses, but he didn't care and it didn't bother him as long as his own agenda was taken care of!

I thought, "By leaving me without a penny, he would have manipulated the situation and made me believe that I would have been safe if I moved with them because I had no money."

My father thought that he still had control over me after making me vulnerable and once I had moved with them, he would have gone to prison with my mother and I wouldn't have been able to walk away from the responsibility which he had always planned to give me.

I overheard a conversation between my father and younger brother which allowed me to understand his desperation to sell the house after knowing that he could never control me ever again.

"I have to protect your mum now," my father said.

After my father realised how serious I was about taking them to court if they tried to hurt me again, he felt that he needed to save my mother from what she had done because if I was to take them to court, then the whole truth would have come out in the open.

As the New Year approached, I knew what my plans were for my business and couldn't wait to get started! Even though I experienced such uncertain moments, I felt happy because I didn't need to find anymore answers about why I suffered so much.

My father didn't make things easier because he spoke behind my back and even though he wouldn't say it to my face, he would accuse me of things which weren't my fault. I also realised that he wouldn't stop giving me evil looks even when I told him in the letter that I would take him to court if he was to give me an evil look.

In the past, my father has said something like, "I would be so happy in prison because I wouldn't have bills to worry about. I would have a bed to sleep in, food to eat and it would be nice. Your younger brothers will be okay because social services will look after them."

By reminding myself of this, I realised that my father didn't care about what would have happened to him and the people who would have suffered if I took my parents to court would have been my younger brothers and myself. After realising this, I had to change the way I thought and instead of letting my father's evil looks and words take me off track, I allowed it to motivate me.

2018 had now arrived and before starting work, I already knew that it was the year where my life would come together.

I worked on two projects which were my signature audio programme and self-published book. It wasn't easy to work on both projects because patience is something that I have always disliked and I knew that I needed to have a lot of it if I wanted to complete both projects in time for their launch.

The way I made things easier was by working on each project a week at a time and this allowed me to give the same amount of commitment to each project.

Everything was going great and then I received a phone call from a police officer who wanted to speak. It was about a letter that my father had sent to the police which stated how him and his family had suffered thirty years of harassment and car crime from the neighbours.

As I had lived in the same house during the years car crime was happening including other incidents such as arguments with the neighbours, the police officers wanted to build a bigger picture of what my father had written in the letter. This was the only time when I was asked by the police about what I had experienced without me reporting anything myself.

When my mother was on trial for what she did, the court should have asked to speak with me because I had always lived in the same house and because they didn't ask me, my parents smiled all the way while knowing that they made everyone in the courtroom look like a clown. If this is how unhelpful the justice system is where criminals will get away with destroying lives, then what's the point of having a justice system for historical cases?

Throughout the year, there were so many high and low moments with various uncertainties which made me experience all kinds of emotions, feelings and thoughts. I learnt so many life lessons both the easy and hard way. This is another thing which I have realised about life. If you cannot learn a certain life lesson the easy way, then you will have to learn it the hard way.

There were even moments where I felt like closing my business and getting a retail job because it felt easier. Whenever I experienced a negative emotion, feeling or thought, I reminded myself why I decided to change lives which allowed me to reassure myself of the importance of not giving up.

As I got towards the end of completing my audio programme, I experienced such a powerful moment where I understood why it had to be transformed into a coaching programme where I will work directly with my clients.

I realised that any service which I will offer, it will always involve a direct approach because the way that I am able to bring change into people's lives, it will always be the most impactful with my physical presence.

As I had to renew my legal documents, I decided to remove my middle name at the same time even though I had originally planned to remove it once I had got my own place.

I thought, "Once I have my own place, I can remove my middle name and update my address at the same time to make it feel like a new beginning."

As I already knew that life is very unpredictable, I always kept an open mind because your life can change within the next second! It seemed like a better option to remove my middle name before I got my own place because that way, I will be entering my very own home with being who I am and not with my father included.

When you have been controlled by someone for so many years, you will get to a point where you want them out of your life for good and this is the main reason why I felt so strongly about removing my middle name because it was my father's name.

After realising how much pain he had caused me, he wasn't welcome in my life any longer and will never be a part of my life ever again! By removing my middle name, I created my own identity and the person who I am now is the person who I choose to be!

It felt amazing after I made this change and I realised how important it is to do what you feel right because at the end of the day, only you know what will make you happy.

I always felt so strongly about becoming my own person and never becoming my father because after realising who he truly was and how much he had hurt me, I never wanted any of his evil influences to be part of my new life.

When I think about it now, I haven't ever had a place where I have called home because while I was still living at my parents house, I always felt trapped and suffocated which shouldn't be felt when you're at home.

As I was born into a family where crime was the main motive for my parents, it felt like I was living in a torture chamber where no one knew what was really going on.

I suppose it's like that for many other people where the outside of their house looks all normal yet what is going on inside of the house, it will be a very dark secret that only a few people will be aware of.

Towards the end of the year, each project that I worked on had a separate launch date. As I chose my birthday to be the date of my rebirth and to also launch my business, it will always remain an anniversary both personally and professionally, so on Saturday 22nd September 2018, I launched my new coaching programme **Discovering The Life That You Truly Desire** which transforms a person's entire life. It allows them to break away from their past completely in order to start living their new beginning by giving it their very own meaning.

The 28th November has always been a very emotional date for me because I almost took my life on this day in 2011 and also made a commitment to myself in finding the truth no matter what I had to face even if it was death.

I self-published my book **ALMOST** on Wednesday 28th November 2018 because it was now time to give this date a safe closure. What made it even more emotional is that after so many years of unbearable pain that almost killed me six times, I finally told my story to the whole world where my parents and eldest brother will NEVER be able to deny the truth ever again!

I wonder what else I will achieve in this life?

Chapter Two

Living In Hell

Experiencing trauma and then having to deal with such a painful journey before recovering is like being put to sleep, taken to another planet and then left there to look after yourself. For so many years, I kept asking myself, "where am I?"

"Hey, it's okay. You are here because in order for you to recover, you will have to experience a few years of feeling broken to understand who you don't want to be. You may use alcohol, smoke, or even use drugs and you may even sleep around to just feel like you belong. There will be times where you might even self-harm and the final thought or even action which you might take is suicide. You will have to be strong and I will be here for you because I won't let you destroy yourself. Your life is very important and shouldn't be wasted even though you won't feel alive for a few years."

It would have been so reassuring to have had someone there to say all of those words where I would have understood the journey which I was about to face. It would have allowed me to emotionally and mentally prepare myself where I wouldn't have felt so lost.

There aren't many of us who have had someone there to make us feel safe and to also tell us that we were still human and it wasn't our fault for being someone who we didn't choose to be.

I used to believe that the worst part about the trauma were the moments when it happened. It's not something that I believe anymore because when we have experienced trauma as children, we were too young to understand what happened and when we have experienced trauma as adults, we enter "shock mode" where we aren't able to move during the incident and after even though we may have tried to fight back.

I have accepted that the moment it happens isn't the worst part no matter how many times it may have happened and this is my belief because the way you will cope with what happened, it will be more damaging than the event itself depending on what happened.

It's hard to even understand which scenario would affect someone more. Would it be if they have experienced something as a child and then realise what happened as they grow older or is it by experiencing something as an adult and once the shock has faded away, you realise what happened even though deep down you knew what happened?

I believe that it depends on each individual as we will cope in different ways and how a certain experience will affect one person, it won't affect another in the same way. When I think back to my past, I wasn't aware of what was going on because I felt so lost in every way since my childhood.

When I realised what happened and what was still happening, it didn't affect me as much as I thought it would. What affected me more was having to hear my father deny the abuse that he made me experience. I remember having a conversation with someone where we got to the conclusion of how the emotional abuse had impacted me a lot more than the sexual abuse and I couldn't understand why.

When you have experienced something, the pain which you will feel inside of you will not be seen by others and this hurts the most because you start to believe how no one understands you. By hearing the denial from my father frequently, it affected me so much more because the pain that I felt inside, it was something that only I could understand.

It's difficult to choose only one emotion or feeling out of so many because each emotion and feeling has played a different role and made us experience something unique. If I had to choose one emotion or feeling which remained alive at all times, then it would be feeling broken. I didn't just feel broken emotionally, mentally and physically, I also felt broken spiritually for many years. It felt like I was a walking zombie where I was on a different planet and couldn't understand what life was about.

I couldn't understand how others could smile and laugh where I wasn't always able to do that and the times I would smile or laugh, it would only be to fit in and not be seen as different. One of the biggest behaviours which I learnt to adapt to was wearing a face mask where I always told people "I am fine."

While I was in high school, other students in my class believed that I was gay and I couldn't understand why? It seems like if you're skinny and hanging around with one guy in high school just because you don't like to have a huge group of friends, then you must be gay? Society has developed a way to give a quick judgement on certain scenarios and even though it may not be the truth, you will still be labelled without even being asked if it's the truth.

It's like if a guy was to approach a child to stop them from crying in the street where they didn't know each other. People would start assuming that he would be a perpetrator because this is how society has taught us what to think when we see something.

There is a similar judgement with saying that you're an abuse survivor. There are people who wouldn't want anything to do with an abuse survivor because they still believe that you would become an abuser as you have experienced sexual abuse in the past.

Depending on what we have experienced as not everyone will experience the same thing no matter how similar two different incidents might be, the various beliefs which we will adapt to will also play a huge part in how we would live our life. These beliefs can come from both our own perception about how we were feeling and it can also come from people judging us including the person or people who hurt us.

The biggest belief which I wasn't able to stop from ruling my life for a long time was that I had done something wrong in my last life and now I was suffering because of it. I couldn't make sense of why I would experience such painful trauma and when I researched about past, present and after life, I read comments on how people believed that their suffering had come from doing something bad in their previous life.

The main reason why my father was able to keep me under his control for so long is because he knew how vulnerable I was and from believing whatever he was telling me and the way he kept me fearful against him, he knew that he could rule my life as much as he wanted until I broke out of his control for good.

The biggest part of recovering from years of trauma was to undo the patterns of behaviour, beliefs, emotions and feelings because without doing that, it wouldn't have been possible to break away from the negativity which I had lived in for so many years. When you have lived the same painful life for so many years, it becomes a cycle of self-abuse and without being aware of it; you end up taking ownership of what happened to you because you begin to believe that it was your fault.

What we need to understand is that we are not to blame for how we may have behaved and coped with what we have experienced because it wasn't our fault and we didn't ask for it. We were just living our life when everything became dark. It's like if you imagine yourself in a dark room where you can't see anything. You will end up getting hurt when trying to move around because you don't know what is around you.

This is the same with living in darkness after experiencing trauma because we can't see the light even though we will carry on with trying to live a normal life. To break away from the past, there needs to be a big enough reason.

It's like if you were to get a burglar alarm fitted in your house. The biggest reason which would make you get a burglar alarm would be the safety of you and your family, so you wouldn't care about the price because the pain of being hurt would be more traumatic than the price that you would pay to have it installed.

The biggest reason for breaking free from the past would be how painful it would be to live in the darkness which you would have done for so many years and the thought of not finding who you are truly meant to be and seeing what you can achieve, it would become unbearable which would allow you to gain the strength to become emotionally resilient and once you have decided to start over, nothing will stop you apart from yourself.

The journey of recovering is another painful journey because for you to live without everything that you have experienced, you will need to accept what you experienced and learn to live with it first. "I'm a survivor." Having to say these words and accept yourself as a survivor is the first step of breaking free because you are telling yourself in much deeper words that even though what you have experienced can't ever be changed, what you can change is your present situation and your future.

My journey of recovery wasn't easy because nothing in life is easy. Sometimes, I wanted to give up and not discover who I was meant to be because I didn't have much support around me before 2014 and the little support which I had in 2010, 2011 and 2012; it wasn't something which had continued.

I had so many dreams of what I had experienced and at first; I thought that it was because I wasn't dealing with what happened. The dreams which I experienced were there to help me understand various emotions, feelings and thoughts which I wasn't already aware of consciously.

To help make my situation easier, I wrote poetry and spent time with music which all turned into coping methods from an expression and this is where I stopped doing them. I thought that I could never do them again, until I was at the final stages of my recovery where I realised that I would need to reclaim myself completely, in order to start over and not let my past hold any part of me because my future was more important than thinking about what I had experienced.

As I was still living at my parents' house where the abuse towards me escalated, it made it more difficult to break free because I wasn't aware of why they wanted to control me so much. The moment when I realised why they had been controlling me for so many years, it allowed me to become even more emotionally resilient where I started to form my own actions to break away from their negativity for good.

There were moments where things happened so naturally without me having to do anything. I understood that once you have decided to break away from your past in order to find yourself and be the person that you have always desired to be, your life will give you the strength to overcome every barrier which you may face.

I realised that even though opening the final abuse case wouldn't bring an outcome; it was something that I still needed to do because that's how I would understand my whole situation even better and instead of feeling broken; I felt such power because after being silenced to talk about it for so long; I knew the truth which gave me the courage to not stay quiet any longer!

The arguments which I had with my parents on 24ᵗʰ June 2016 and 1ˢᵗ April 2017, they couldn't have been avoided because they made me realise who I needed to keep out of my life for good and why?

It was hard to accept that I couldn't turn the clock back and make the changes which I thought would have made my recovery journey easier. I knew that I had the strength to break free, so I remained positive because once you have made a commitment to yourself in finding the truth, you will do everything that you can to keep your innocence.

I was nineteen years of age when I had a dream of me running on a train platform as I was being chased and while being in a deep sleep, I wet the bed and woke up feeling very ashamed while thinking, "how will I be able to be with someone because if they are sleeping next to me and I wet the bed, will they even understand?"

The most important years of my life which were my childhood, teenage hood and early adulthood is something that I'll never understand because I didn't live those years. Even though I became a year older each year, I didn't experience those years which is something that I'll always question of how it would have felt?

Even when I will have my own children and see them live through the years that I didn't, it's something which I won't understand because I never lived it. I remember a time in 2011 where I used to stand in front of the window of my house and watch the students walk by. It made me so angry because I never experienced being a teenager. I wonder who I would have become and how my life would have been if I didn't experience any trauma?

I am twenty-six years of age while writing this and I have never had a real life girlfriend and having a social life is something that I have missed out for so many years just because of my father's selfish agenda!

Even though I have missed out on so much, it's not something that I won't ever experience because I will have everything in my future. The only difference is that I didn't experience it during the years that I didn't live.

I never had the space to grow with responsibility in my own time of slowly getting into looking after myself because I always found myself pushed into the responsibility of looking after myself through control.

Before gaining the strength to start speaking, I used to have a technique which would allow me to say something to my father when I needed to and not feel scared. I would count to three and then say what I needed to say. By doing this, it would give me the strength to not be afraid of him even for a few seconds.

Another fear which I overcame was how everything which I heard was directed towards me. Even if I was walking on the street and someone would shout to call someone, I would assume that they would be calling me which would make me shake. This was addressed during my counselling sessions in 2012 and my counsellor made me realise that I had become hypersensitive.

Before overcoming the sexual abuse and how it affected me, I would always walk close to the walls if a guy or a group of guys were walking past me on the street. I would even need space on both sides of my body while I would sit on the sofa at home because by feeling a touch from a guy, it would make me feel so dirty.

It felt good to realise why so many people weren't able to understand me which made me aware of how the countless arguments that I had with my father; they were pointless because even though he knew what he was doing was wrong, he couldn't understand how it was making me feel as he never experienced it from the receiving end. If someone hasn't experienced what you have, then they won't ever be able to understand what it's like.

If someone genuinely cares about you and wants to help, then they can only support you and respect the decisions that you will make because if they haven't experienced something which you have, then they won't know what needs to be done to overcome the experience.

From understanding the journey of change, I became aware of how I needed to know the truth about my past which would allow me to move on. Having peace about my past was so important because I would have continued to live in darkness otherwise. It was also important because I wouldn't have any more questions about it.

By listening to so many empowering stories, I saved myself from self-harming and substance abuse because I knew what would happen if I chose those ways to cope. The only time I used alcohol was in December 2013 during an argument with my father which changed everything for the good because it made me realise how bad things would have got if I didn't do something about my situation.

Even though emotionally and mentally I was suffering so much, I still knew what I needed to stay away from. It seems like being introverted also helped as I wasn't around the wrong people outside and causing trouble.

I also understood that someone who hasn't hurt you, they can remind you of someone who has hurt you. The way they would sit, talk, dress, and so on, it would remind you of the person or people who have hurt you and this would make you hate them even though they wouldn't be to blame for anything. After understanding this, I learnt to control how I felt about various situations and to not let my past affect me in such a way.

My belief in God was very strong when I was younger and I prayed every day. Once my life became very difficult in 2011, I questioned my beliefs in God because I couldn't understand why things were getting worse no matter how many times I prayed?

I thought, "Is God really there or is he just a myth because I have done nothing wrong, so why am I suffering so much? I've made mistakes like everyone but that doesn't make me a bad person. I don't want to hurt people for personal gain like my parents, so why are they allowed to abuse me in such a way and get away with it?"

Sometimes, I have prayed to God when I have felt so alone and scared and this made me question whether God was testing me if he isn't a myth? I am uncertain about my beliefs because I still have a lot to experience in life and maybe those positive experiences will allow me to understand my belief better?

I don't believe in religion completely because it creates a division and hate towards many people from past events. Even though it brings people together and allows them to be part of something, I dislike the way it creates boundaries and how it's used by people to cause harm to others.

Over the past five years, I have become very spiritual, and this is something which makes me happy. There are no limits to success and whatever I put my mind to, it will become a reality if it's meant to be. I know between right and wrong and as I don't have an evil agenda to use people or hurt anyone for my personal gain, I am not afraid of what will happen to me once my time arrives to leave this world.

Many people always say, "you should be afraid of God." If you have done nothing wrong and don't have an evil agenda, then you have got nothing to worry about. Learning about life will always involve emotional distress no matter what area of life it will be. These events are needed for you to grow and it doesn't make you a bad person to experience these events because you are only human at the end of the day.

For things like love, God, and so on, it's always best to let it happen naturally. Forcing things to happen won't give you the outcome because there's always the right time for something. I believe that everything happens for a reason no matter what it is and whoever we will meet whether it's for short-term or long-term, they are all meant to be in our lives during the times we will need them because they are the ones who will teach us what we need to learn.

I've accepted that people will come and go in my life and even when I think that they will stay for good, it may not always be the case. Expecting the unexpected is what I have also accepted because no matter what it is, you won't see it coming. This is why it's healthier to go with the flow and to not focus on planning so much because no matter how much planning you may do, you will never be fully prepared.

Adapting to change is something that is also important because when our life becomes unstable from a certain event, it can leave us shaken up. Most of us dislike change because we don't always enjoy living outside of our comfort zone. I've learnt how important it is to accept change because whatever is meant to be, it will be.

No matter how hard life got for me, there was always one thought which reassured me. "If I have done nothing wrong and I don't have a plan to do anything wrong, then I have nothing to worry about because whatever will happen in my life, it will be for the positive. The worst has already happened, so everything that I will experience now, it will help me grow in every way."

The biggest form of understanding which I experienced, it involved meeting my inner child. There was a time in 2014 towards the end of the Team programme where I was having a shower and saw myself as a child and as a teenager where I kept saying, "God, what did you have to go through Shikesh?" It felt like I was watching a movie of myself where I understood something much bigger which allowed me to understand my past in such simple words.

I was holding my inner child's hand while we were walking on a train track and the moment when I experienced trauma for the first time, my inner child wasn't holding my hand anymore because we both started walking in different directions. For so many years, he was shouting out yet I couldn't hear his voice because I was too lost and broken to understand what he was saying.

When I was ready to break away from my past in order to start living the life that I have always desired to have, I walked on the same track and called out for my inner child. He ran towards me and gave me the biggest hug while he told me how much he loved me. We both cried in such relief of finding each other before going home. As he knew that I could now understand him, he explained why he had to walk in a different direction

"If I stayed, then I would have also become broken and you would have lost yourself completely. During the time you were broken, I did everything to protect you and that's why you had to become someone who you didn't want to be because it was the only way that you would realise what had happened to you. I knew that you would find me and understand what I was saying because I never gave up on you. Everything that you have always loved doing, I kept it all safe and I will now help you to reclaim your whole life where you won't feel broken ever again!"

He then stood up and held my hand as he took me to a room which was locked. It felt like he was waiting for me to say the password and I already knew what it was.

"I will never be broken ever again!"

The door then opened and while still holding my hand, he took me into the room where there were so many paintings on the walls and they all showed who I truly am. He hugged me again and as he told me how much he loves me, we walked through another door.

I could see my whole future and in that same moment, my inner child said, "you don't have to look for yourself anymore or feel lost or confused because you already know who you truly are."

Chapter Three

Who, How & Why?

After any event, the time arrives to look back and analyse everything that happened. This is very important because in order to stop the same event from happening twice, essential lessons will need to be learnt on who was involved, how it happened and why it happened?

My mission in knowing who was responsible and why they abused me for so long was already known. What I wasn't aware of was how could it have gone on for twenty years where no one was there to stop it?

The main person who is responsible for masterminding the whole plan is my father. The people who are responsible for hurting me and supporting my father are both my mother and my eldest brother. All three of them are blood related as I haven't ever had any adopted, foster or step parents or siblings.

Even though people outside of the family have hurt me, I don't see them as being responsible for how long I have had to suffer because if my family didn't put me through what they did, then I wouldn't have had to endure such pain until twenty-seven years of age.

I never had to experience twenty years of abuse and the reason it happened was because my father wanted to use me to achieve his own selfish agenda. Everything that he said and did from my childhood until I was twenty-seven, it was to keep me under his control so he could hurt people and go to prison with my mother while knowing that I was at home looking after the house and my younger brothers. He learnt what he needed to say and do to control me by supporting survivors in the past when he was volunteering.

The moment when I broke out of his control and came to know the truth, he wanted to make sure that I didn't expose him so he spread lies, made me look bad and threatened to make me homeless if I spoke the truth. He became so desperate to keep me quiet and he achieved this for a few weeks with the support of my mother.

When my mother realised that she wouldn't be able to cope with being a single mother, she supported my father and betrayed me because she wanted to make sure that she didn't struggle and even though she knew that my father was the problem; she didn't care about living under his control as it became her normal living.

They controlled me in a way where they made me believe that I was planning for my future when in fact; they were waiting for the right moment to go to prison and then tell me what they wanted me to do. This is why my father wanted me to find a job when I was depressed and suicidal because all he cared about was his own agenda.

When I called the ambulance and was attending counselling, he made it seem like he cared when, really; he was just waiting until I had recovered so he could start his control again which he did. By having made a commitment to myself of wanting to know why I suffered so much, it took my parents off guard. As they didn't know about my intentions, they ended up making mistakes and this is how they got caught because there is no such thing as a perfect crime.

My eldest brother abused me because he wanted to feel quick pleasure by watching porn which his friend had shown him and the reason why he listened to my father rather than thinking about how his actions would hurt me, it was because he didn't care about me and from how he treated me, my father was able to brainwash me further during the emotional abuse for money.

I couldn't understand why my father wanted to harm people who he believed were part of a "paedophile ring." The theories which he has told me has been his own perception and not the truth, so why did he create a diversion story?

He has always spoken about his father and how everything that he has done has been because of his father. In 1999 when his father was in the hospital in India, he didn't go to him because my mother told him to wait for two weeks as we were all going together.

Within those two weeks, his father passed away, and it seems like he hasn't dealt with it ever since. I keep questioning whether he is still holding the guilt because of it and if so, is he blaming other people just because he doesn't want to take the blame? My parents have never got on with their families, so they have always been at war.

Everything that my father has told me about them has been his words and I haven't heard the other side of the story, so I don't know the truth about what really happened between them.

If my father wanted to hurt people just because he doesn't want to take the responsibility of not being with his father when he was in hospital and he wants to blame others instead, then it just shows what guilt can do to you if you don't accept the truth.

For my father to tell my mother how she also needed to hurt people, it could be because she stopped my father from going, so he felt that she needed to make up for not allowing him to go to his father when he needed him? My father had a choice, and no one stopped him from going, so it was his own decision even when my mother told him to wait.

Whatever my parents agenda was, they tried to use me to achieve it and they didn't care about my life. Everything that I was planning for my future, my father made sure that it didn't happen because he wanted me to stay at home as he felt that he wouldn't have been able to achieve his goal otherwise.

This is why I suffered for twenty years and no other reason. It's because my parents took my life away from me as they wanted someone at home to look after their younger kids and the house while they were in prison. I was always loyal to them, so my father knew that he could use it against me and also make me feel guilty about various situations which were just a theory. Once they realised that it wasn't possible to use me anymore, they agreed that it was best to either make me homeless or send me to prison by framing me.

If either of those scenarios occurred, then they would have made up their own story and no one would have believed me. The only thing that they didn't want was for me to commit suicide because if that had happened, then there would have been an investigation where the truth would have been revealed, so this is why they wanted me homeless or in prison and not dead, even though my father threatened my life on various occasions.

The way that everything happened in my life during my recovery journey, it was perfect for me because I had a lot of free time to myself and even though I was completing courses and volunteering; I wasn't busy every single day. This gave me a lot of time to think and reflect on what had happened and what was still happening.

By having the free time that I did, I understood the whole situation, and this is how I came to know the truth. If I had got a job and focused on saving up and moving out, then I wouldn't have known the truth and from the way that my father had controlled me, he would have found another way to stop me from leaving if I worked to save up in order to find a place of my own before breaking away from his control.

As I look back now, my father would have hurt someone and gone to prison before I would have even left home and as I didn't know the whole truth and was still in his control until the beginning of 2016, I know I wouldn't have realised the truth for a very long time. All my father wanted was for me to have a job because that way, he would have been reassured of knowing that I was getting an income and would have been able to pay the bills and look after my younger brothers.

After experiencing my recovery journey, I learnt how important it is to trust the journey because even though you may not enjoy what might happen, your end goal will always be achieved. The way we will reach our end goal may not happen in the same way of how we imagined it and it's not because our life is punishing us, no. It's because the way we will experience the journey, it will teach us the life lessons and skills that we would need in order to prepare for the outcome.

If there is such a thing as being possessed and if my eldest brother was possessed to abuse me, then something about him would have been different and noticeable. If I had to give my personal opinion on spirit possession, then I would say that it would be like being on some drug where you wouldn't be your full self and it would be noticeable.

During the sexual abuse from my eldest brother, there was nothing different about him and he was normal, apart from what he did of course. With my father brainwashing me about my eldest brother being possessed, it was a cover-up story to keep me quiet so I would never speak about it. This wasn't the outcome because you cannot keep someone under your control for good.

From various experiences which might be seen as paranormal by many people who believe in witchcraft, I would say that anything is possible, however, as I haven't experienced many paranormal or spirit possession experiences, I cannot believe in it or empathise with it because in order to understand something fully, you will have to experience it yourself.

The day that I broke free from my parents' control and my past, it wasn't the day that I recovered. It was the day I started to speak because by having a voice; I spoke up for myself and didn't stay quiet which allowed me to express how I felt. I was able to ask for help which gave me more strength to carry on where I spoke for others also and lastly; I told my story and kept my innocence.

The final question which now remains is how weren't my parents ever caught by the authorities until I exposed them? There are two reasons why both of my parents were never caught by the authorities until I exposed them.

The first reason is because my father knows the system very well which has always given him the upper hand of playing along to not get caught. This is why my mother got away with what she did because my father guided her every step of the way in order to remain innocent in the eyes of others when really, she is guilty and so is my father for masterminding the plan which shouldn't have ever happened.

The second reason why my parents never got caught by the authorities is because the police, CPS and social services have missed the **WARNING SIGNS.** When you have experienced twenty years of abuse, you think long and hard about why the authorities are always missing the **WARNING SIGNS?** My conclusion is because there is not enough **EMPATHY** and the procedures of how the system works, it needs to be updated.

It doesn't matter how much training you have completed and how long you have been in the job. If you haven't experienced anything similar yourself that you are dealing with on the job, then you can never understand what is really going on when it comes to historical abuse. The people who will be responsible for the abuse won't always get caught because of this.

This is the same for schools and mental health where if you haven't experienced anything similar yourself that you may deal with on the job, then you will not be able to understand what is really going on because you will be looking through the wrong pair of glasses and therefore, you will be blinded.

I will now share various scenarios of what I have experienced, so you can understand at what moments the abuse could have been prevented and the moments where both of my parents would have been caught if the **WARNING SIGNS** had been noticed by the authorities.

Scenario one: Being told that both of my friends and myself were too young to go to court when I almost got run over.

Does this mean that any child who experiences something under the age of twelve is unreliable and therefore, their voices wouldn't be heard? I am sure that there have been many improvements within the justice system throughout the years since it happened. Every child from five years of age and above should be given the opportunity to have their voices heard where they are fully supported throughout.

Scenario two: My teachers assumed that I was a good boy for always being quiet.

There have been many changes within schools throughout the years to safeguard better. It is essential that safeguarding remains an ongoing training in every aspect to identify a concern which may arise in a child's/young person's life.

Scenario three: My father told me to swear at the neighbour living in front of us for not moving their car.

The community needs to build a strong relationship and neighbours need to have an open-mind when they witness something. Even though every neighbour will not report everything that they will see, it's still important to do so because this is how abuse can also be identified and more importantly, prevented!

An example is the 2nd April 2017 when I went for a walk. While I was walking back home and before I walked into the driveway, the neighbour living beside me who locked the cat in his garage said hello. I didn't reply or look at him because of past disagreements and this was the first time when he said hello in a very long time.

I knew that he had heard the five-hour argument the day before and wanted to talk about it. If he had heard words such as "sexual abuse" while knowing that I have younger brothers, then he should have reported it because it would have helped a lot.

Scenario four: The times when social services have been involved in my life and my brothers lives, our father has prepared us on what to say and what not to say.

When it comes to investigating a report about a child/young person, there needs to be a full investigation which leaves out any "what if" questions. After experiencing everything that I have for several years, I have understood what I feel needs to be improved.

1: A way to understand if a child/young person has been told what to say. This can be by asking them various questions to identify if they are saying something which they have been told to say.

2: The social services should interview every single person who is living with the child/young person whether they are over eighteen years of age or not including the neighbours. The way that my father has abused me, he has never abused my younger brothers in such a way. Saying that, they were brainwashed to believe something else, so they didn't understand the unsafe environment that they were living in because it became their normal living. If the social services had interviewed me when my younger brothers were being investigated, then they would have known the truth about my parents.

3: The house needs to be observed fully both inside and outside. If the social services had interviewed me, then they would have known why the front and back garden was in such a mess. My father had left an open entrance into the back garden by removing the fences and it remained like that for two years.

If I was a social worker carrying out an observation, then I would find it unsafe for the child/young person because if they were playing in the garden, then anyone could walk in. The front and back garden are also the living environment, so they must be safe also and not just the inside of the house.

4: A doctor/nurse should be present with social services and the police if a report has been made about a child being abused. This would identify any abuse such as bruises covered up with make-up and it would also prevent further harm to the child/young person after the authorities have visited.

Scenario five: The mental health services were asking my father to take medication for being delusional.

If the mental health services are visiting the house and asking my father to take medication because he is delusional from the type of cases that he was reporting to the police, then shouldn't the social services have been informed about the safety of my brothers and myself?

If I was working in the mental health services and I visited a house where the father may be delusional, then I would think, "what if he is telling his children things that they shouldn't be hearing?"

Scenario six: A chief of police visited my eldest brother at work after I called the ambulance to save my life.

Why wasn't my father interviewed by the same chief of police because he was the reason why I almost took my life? Even though my eldest brother benefited with my money, he wasn't the reason why I almost took my life.

A full investigation should take place to make sure that it doesn't happen again and every single person who is responsible for making someone feel such a way, they should be investigated because in my eyes, any type of abuse no matter how small it might seem is highly unacceptable.

The social services should also be informed because if there are any children/young people living in the house during any form of abuse, then everyone's safety/well-being should be a priority!

Scenario seven: When I reported the sexual abuse case in 2016 about my eldest brother, the police took no report about my father's carbon monoxide poisoning theory.

Even though the police officers believed that it was too hard to prove, I feel that a report should have been taken and an investigation should have been carried out. An investigation shouldn't just be about facts and evidence, it should also be about how something or someone has made a person feel because a person's emotional and mental well-being should always come first!

I didn't believe the theory fully because I had realised that my father wasn't right about many things. Saying that, it still affected me so much and this is what the police would have come to know if they had taken a statement and investigated it further.

There is something called **Project Violet** where if any words relating to witchcraft are mentioned during a report, then police officers would be sent to the house **IMMEDIATELY** to safeguard everyone. Why didn't any police officers contact me to ask about what I had said? Could this have been in a breakdown of communication or did the police not care about what I had said?

Scenario eight: When I called the police on the 24th June 2016 during an argument with my father.

On the 15th September 2017 after I gave my father the money to remove the repossession order, he told me that social services had contacted him to ask about the argument which took place.

If my father isn't making up another story and social services contacted him, then why didn't they speak to me directly if they wanted to know why I was arguing and as the police would have informed the social services, they would have known of the things that I had said?

On the day of the argument, the lady police officer told me not to argue while standing beside her. What if I was going to expose my parents by telling the police what was really happening and by being told not to argue, I became silenced out of fear? Unless a person is behaving in a way where they will hurt someone, they should be allowed to speak and not be told to stay quiet.

The way that you can make someone homeless so easily just because it's your house is not acceptable in my eyes. I believe that there should be a court procedure where if the owner wishes for someone to leave their house forcefully, then this should be the appropriate method than just kicking them out and if they have been violent, then it's understandable that they would be arrested. Either way, there should be a court procedure.

If at the end of the court case the outcome is the person has to leave, then there should be support for them to have a place ready to move into depending on their financial circumstances because if they have no money to move into a place of their own, stay in a B&B, hostel and so on, then they would have no other choice but to live on the streets if they have no other support from family or friends.

I would have been able to speak the truth about what was really happening and why I was being threatened with being homeless if a court procedure was in place. In my personal and professional opinion, this should become a law!

Scenario nine: After my youngest brother's school offered him counselling, my parents transferred him to another school.

This should have been investigated further because if parents/guardians have nothing to hide, then why would they refuse their child/young person to attend counselling? If a school offers counselling to a child/young person and they then move to another school, shouldn't this be a **RED ALERT?**

My youngest brother changed to two different schools within a year and the social services were involved at the same time. The only thing that didn't happen was me being interviewed?

Scenario ten: My father told my youngest brother to call another boy in his school "an evil person" and when he heard that his "uncle" was picking him up, he ran out of school and came home himself.

Even though my youngest brother got bullied in his last lesson, shouldn't the teachers have known that a child who is bullied, they will never run from a teacher if he/she is being picked up by their parents/guardians every day, so why did he run when he heard that his "uncle" was picking him up?

When the deputy head teacher heard the whole conversation over the phone once my youngest brother had arrived at home, shouldn't he have seen my parents and asked them about what he had heard?

I believe that the social services should have been involved and I should have been interviewed! Even though many schools around the UK have strengthened their safeguarding, it just shows that it's not enough and I'll say it again, you won't ever be able to understand what is happening if you are looking through the wrong pair of glasses.

Scenario eleven: My mother attacked my father's eldest brother.

There was a time during the trial when my mother took both of my younger brothers to see her solicitor.

Now that I know what my mother always meant when she kept on saying "you're not well, just look after yourself," I wouldn't be surprised if she spread a lie to make everyone else believe that I was depressed and had mental health problems, so I wouldn't be fit to attend court.

When there is a case which involves historical aspects, every single person within the family should be interviewed whether they have mental health problems or not. Even if they are not fit to attend court, they should still be interviewed and their statement should be read in court because every person's voice is important!

I have had a lot of time to reflect and think about the times when I would have been saved if the authorities had noticed the **WARNING SIGNS.** Some may ask me if I am angry at the authorities because they have missed eleven opportunities!

I am not angry because if someone hasn't experienced something similar, then they won't ever be able to understand, so I cannot be angry or hold any blame towards the authorities. Saying that, I know there are people on the job who don't care because they only want the money and status.

I am only frustrated at how the system is because even to this day. children are dying after the authorities have visited the house. The only thing which brings me peace when thinking about such pain within my life and so many others' lives is that there is a solution!

The biggest way that change can happen is for the authorities to work with survivors and to understand how every type of scenario can be dealt with appropriately which will help identify concerns that may not be seen otherwise.

I'll say it again, if you haven't experienced anything similar personally which you will deal with on the job, then you will not be able to understand what has happened or what might even still be happening.

It was my decision to stay alive and find out the truth because I didn't want to take my life without knowing why I had to suffer for so many years? How could I have been born where all I ever experienced was abuse until twenty-seven years of age?

It would have been an easy decision for me to take my life because the easy way out always seems the better option as you wouldn't experience suffering any longer or would you? It all depends on your beliefs about life and death.

There are so many people in the world where right this second, they are being abused, raped, beaten, killed and many other things and we cannot do anything about it to stop it this second. It makes me so angry by knowing how much suffering is in the world because no one should ever have to suffer just because of someone else's selfish agenda!

What we can do is raise awareness and keep on raising awareness by talking louder and **LOUDER!** We shouldn't be afraid of what people will think because we have a voice for a reason! If we have something to say, then we should say it! If we will not speak up and share our pain, then what's the point of even talking about world peace?

By speaking, raising awareness and teaching each other on how we can better safeguard ourselves and everyone else on this earth even though such evil crimes may not be stopped fully, the percentage of it will be minimised and eventually, future generations could live in a world where they won't have to put up a guard just to feel safe within their own skin.

I think about my life every day because I am always improving myself in every way that I can. I also think about what my life would have been like if I didn't experience abuse and it leaves me coming back to the same conclusion that maybe I was chosen for this life because after experiencing twenty years of trauma and how I am still alive and so sane, there must be a reason for it?

There are many moments when I think about all of the decisions that I made and if I could have changed anything? I then remind myself that everything happens for a reason and there is no such thing as a coincidence in my eyes. As I look back to all of the moments of how each traumatic event began, I seem to come back to the same evaluation of knowing that I couldn't have done anything different because everything that I have learnt, it wouldn't have been possible if I didn't experience it all in the ways that I did.

It all happened so naturally and even when I was panicking while feeling so fearful, I always trusted my gut instincts and they never let me down because my gut instincts will always be the voice of my inner child. There have been moments where I haven't listened to my gut instincts so I could understand what would happen. It wasn't a good idea because by not listening to my inner child; I brought myself more pain.

Even though I didn't have the best start to life, I don't feel left out because we all experience life in our own unique way and as I have suffered a lot during the years that I did, I won't ever suffer in such ways again. I will now be able to live my life and have happiness in my own unique way by making the right choices and not wrong.

By experiencing the life lessons that I have learnt and from teaching myself how to break away from a negative past in order to live an amazing future, I have gained the necessary skills needed to help others do the same. Once I realised why I had suffered so much, I could have still taken my life because the pain that I felt, it wasn't easy to accept.

Instead, I lived and dedicated my life to helping others because I know what needs to be done and how. Many people believe that if you focus on your own life and find your own happiness, then you are selfish? I disagree because we are all born to be unique and not live someone else's life. If I had taken my life after discovering the truth while knowing that I had the solution to help people, then I wouldn't have argued with anyone for being called selfish.

It's been a really tough journey and being suicidal six times year after year, it was a very dark road that I walked on. I have literally drained so much sweat, blood and tears over the years from everything that I have experienced and even though I have lost so much, I have gained so much more.

The way that I view my life now isn't in a negative way anymore because even though I didn't do well at school or go to university, everything that I have experienced is my qualification and experience where I am now fully qualified to do my job of helping people change their lives for the better also.

Who I am in my personal life is who I am in my professional life, so I don't even need to get into work mode. I don't even see myself as having a job because I don't feel like I am working. I am living my dreams every single day and to see a smile on someone's face and their reaction when they experience a lightbulb moment; it was worth the suffering that I endured.

At the end of my painful life, I gave myself a rebirth to turn it all around into something so magical and no matter what will happen in my life from now, it will all be a positive to keep me growing.

Chapter Four

It Speaks For Itself

It felt amazing to think about how my innocence could be proven and after finding some very important evidence, I knew that my side of the story wasn't just going to be words.

You will see various images of my parents diaries, and so on, that will show what has happened and how my parents have treated me over the years. I have blacked out sensitive information such as names of people and places. I will give a short explanation under each image so it's easier to understand.

The images below are from my father's diary.

"Shikesh again broke his silence so good for him God help him."

This is when I told my parents about the sexual abuse that my eldest brother made me experience.

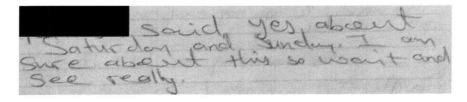

"Eldest son said yes about Saturday and Sunday. I am sure about this so wait and see really."

This is when my eldest brother admitted to sexually abusing me when my father asked him about it in front of me.

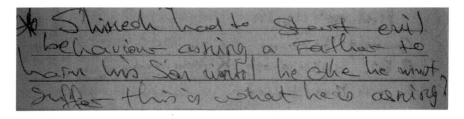

"Shikesh had to start evil behaviour asking a father to harm his son until he die he must suffer this is what he is asking?"

My father has been wanting to harm people just because he blames them for how his life turned out. If I want justice for what my eldest brother did to me by having him investigated, then it's an evil behaviour for wanting to live my human rights? Whenever I have shared my views with my father, he has blown them out of proportion and turned them into his own conclusions.

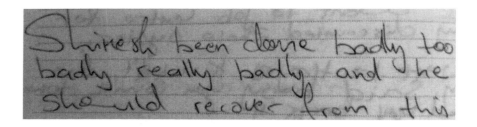

"Shikesh been done badly too badly really badly and he should recover from this."

Whenever I became upset or angry from my father's emotional abuse, he would make me believe that the "paedophile ring" were doing witchcraft on me and that's why I was feeling the way I was.

He would make me believe that the only way to recover from it was by listening to him and doing whatever he was telling me to do, such as letting him take my money without a question and not arguing with him if he didn't pay me back.

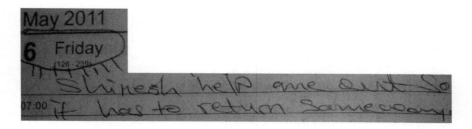

"Shikesh help me out so it has to return same way."

This is when I received the compensation and through intimidation, he made me give him two thousands pounds. My father has always made the emotional abuse seem like "I helped him out because I wanted to" which was never the case. This is how he has controlled me by playing with my generosity and loyalty.

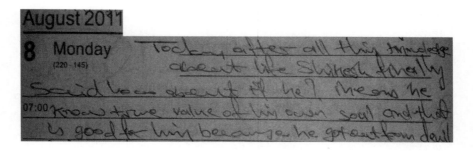

"Today after all this knowledge about life Shikesh finally said how about if he? Means he know true value of his own soul and that is good for him because he got out from devil."

My father had made me believe that if he lost the house, then it would have been my fault, so I paid one thousand pounds to the mortgage company. Just because I offered the money with my own words from the fears that my father had made me believe, I got out from the devil's control?

The mortgage guy told me not to pay anymore because it was my parents' mortgage, so my father made me withdraw one thousand pounds before putting it into his account. This made it look like he was paying it and not me.

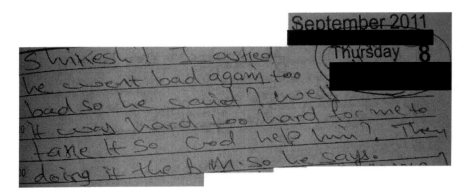

"Shikesh? I asked he went bad again too bad so he said? Well it was hard too hard for me to take it so God help him? They doing it the B.M so he says."

Once I began believing my father's words that I was being control through witchcraft to not give my father my money, he made it seem like it was my own belief and he never made me believe such a thing. B.M stands for black magic.

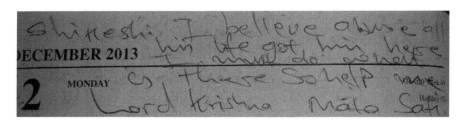

"Shikesh: I believe abuse all his life got him here. I must do what is there so help me Lord Krishna Mata Sati."

"I must do what is there." This basically means that my father must harm the people who he believed were the reason for how my life was. Lord Krishna is a Hindu God and Mata Sati is my father's ancestors.

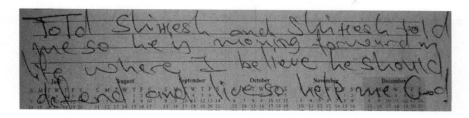

"Told Shikesh and Shikesh told me so he is moving forward in life where I believe he should defend and live so help me God."

This shows my father's views of believing that I needed to hurt people because that was the only way how I could live safely?

"Shikesh said yes to fee for Gas Safe. God Bless to him one step forward now."

This is when he told me to give him four hundred pounds at the end of December 2013. After an argument with him, I decided to change my life and enroll onto The Prince's Trust Team Programme.

Whenever my father has used me to achieve whatever he wanted, he would move forward with his own life and I would end up moving ten steps back. This is how he always kept me until I decided to take a stand and stay standing.

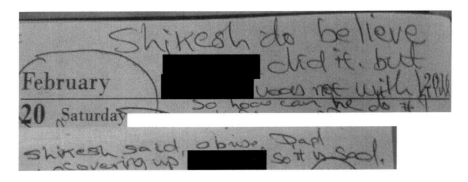

"Shikesh do believe his eldest brother did it, but his eldest brother was not with him so how can he do it? Shikesh said, abuse Dad covering up his eldest son so it is sad."

This is when I reported my eldest brother in 2016 for what he made me experience at twelve years of age.

If my father was really genuine, then he would have said something like, "I wasn't there, so I don't know what happened and what didn't. I know my son wouldn't lie about such a thing."

Instead, he claims that my eldest brother wasn't even with me? If both of my parents were away for the weekend to see the psychic, then how do they know what happened and what didn't?

Throughout the whole investigation, my parents emotionally abused me, intimidated me and provoked me on several occasions just to keep me weak. If my father informed my eldest brother about what was coming towards him and he told him what to say and what not to say to get away with it, then isn't that a cover-up, especially when my father heard the confession himself?

The way that my father has acted by making every scenario look so innocent and genuine, he felt that he would never get caught for what has really been happening.

"Shikesh is scumbag believes he suffering."

This was the day when my mother came home from court after attacking my father's eldest brother. My father has always told the police how his kids have been in danger, so he has been trying to protect them because people outside of the family have tried to harm them?

If this was true, then why would my father even believe such a thing? The fact is, I haven't ever believed that I have been suffering. This is because I know that I have been suffering as I have experienced many different traumatic events for twenty years!

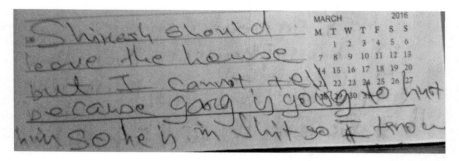

"Shikesh should leave the house but I cannot tell because gang is going to hurt him so he is in shit so I know."

This is what my father has always told me how I wouldn't be safe if I had my own place unless he had done something to protect me? If this was the case, then why did he allow my eldest brother to get his own place? My eldest brother has never been controlled in the way I have and I always wondered why he was treated better than me?

This was written a month after I reported my eldest brother to the police. When I said nothing and kept my mouth shut, my father gave me no threats. Once I started talking about the truth, my father became the most evil-minded person that I have ever met in my life!

I have been wanting to leave and get my own place since 2010. The way my father controlled me and how much money he has taken from me, it wasn't possible for me to go. Once I realised that my father was to blame, I stayed in his house myself because that was the only way I could understand what had really happened and why.

I am so glad that I didn't leave because if I had left without knowing the whole truth, then I would have always felt trapped.

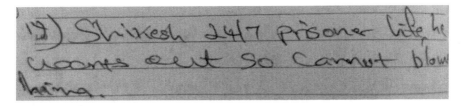

"Shikesh 24/7 prisoner life, he wants out so cannot blame him."

After everything that my father has put me through, he empathises with how my life has been? This just shows how guilty my father is because from all of the control and lies that he has told about me, for him to write what he has in the above image, it proves that I haven't been the problem.

The images below are from my mother's diary.

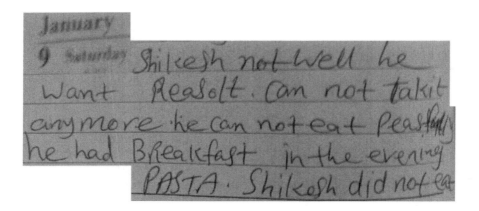

"Today Shikesh did not eat anything."

"Shikesh not well he want result. Cannot take it anymore. He cannot eat peacefully, he had Breakfast. In the evening PASTA. Shikesh did not eat."

This was during the start of 2016 when I was physically sick from knowing that my father didn't keep his promise about doing something. I wasn't aware of the truth at this point, so I assumed that my life was still on hold and how I couldn't build a future.

"He want result." This means that I wanted my father to do something because he always made me believe that I wouldn't be able to live my life otherwise.

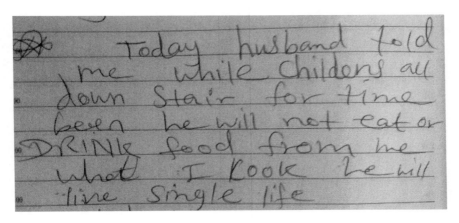

"Today husband told me while childrens all downstairs for time being he will not eat or DRINK food from me. What I cook he will live single life."

If my father didn't have an agenda, then why would he even dare to tell his own wife that he wouldn't eat or drink anything from her for the time being, especially in front of his own kids? Nothing had happened, so they were still talking. My father has always made a scene in front of me and my brothers.

As my father wanted to prove to me that he was serious about hurting people, he wanted to mentally prepare himself for prison. There is no other reason why he would choose to do this.

The image below is of my Job Seeker's Allowance appointment card.

DAY:	DATE:	TIME:	ADVISER:
Tues	3/11/11	10.35	
Thurs	17-11-11	14.10	
Mon	28-11-11	14:15	

APPOINTMENT CARD

PERSONAL ADVISER:

I signed on at the Job Centre twice and on the day of my review meeting; I wasn't there because I called an ambulance to save my life.

I just wonder how my review meeting would have gone? More importantly, I just wonder what would have happened if I had walked out of the house that day with the intention to take my life?

I am uncertain about my beliefs on what happens after death and the way I have suffered and how I am still well; I keep coming back to the same conclusion that maybe I was born for this life?

How can a person be born where they suffer so much for twenty years and then they decide to find the truth before dedicating their life to bringing huge positive changes into the world?

If I didn't choose this life, then it's a miracle that I am still alive because after experiencing so much trauma and not even having a life for twenty-six years, how can you even get your head around that?

As I will start to experience more positive life events, I know that my beliefs about life and death will become more clearer to me.

The image below shows the letter that my parents signed when they were given a repossession notice.

Date: 11/09/2017

RE: Borrowing

This letter is a binding contract from ████████████████████ to person name Shikesh Sorathia who is a second child of owner of ████████████████████ who given fund started from September 2009 to present day.

The sums which been given is mainly to pay mortgage due to ████████████████ time to time so the ████████████████████████ do not get repossessed.

The amount is with interest due is around £30,000. It must be paid on sale of this premises before any money comes to account of the above name owners ████████████████████

This is a legal document sign by both owners ████████████████████

The payment due to Shikesh Sorathia must be made by Bank Draft or a Cheque once ███████ ████████████████████ mortgage and secured loan is cleared.

Almost everything that is written in this letter is a lie because my parents never borrowed any money from me. This is because they took it from me by emotionally abusing me.

They never sat down with me and discussed how much I would be paid back and to even discuss signing a contract with me, it was never mentioned. Just because my parents signed the letter after writing so many lies, it's not a "legal document" in my eyes.

My parents believed that if they manipulated the situation, then they would get away with years of abuse. The only thing that states the truth is how long they have benefited with my money.

Even though they have lied about how the money went to them, my bank statements show different because for a parent to leave their child without a penny where they weren't able to live their life including finding work, it is nothing but abuse! If I had given the money myself, then I wouldn't have been suicidal and called an ambulance to be saved.

The image below shows the right side of my mother's face.

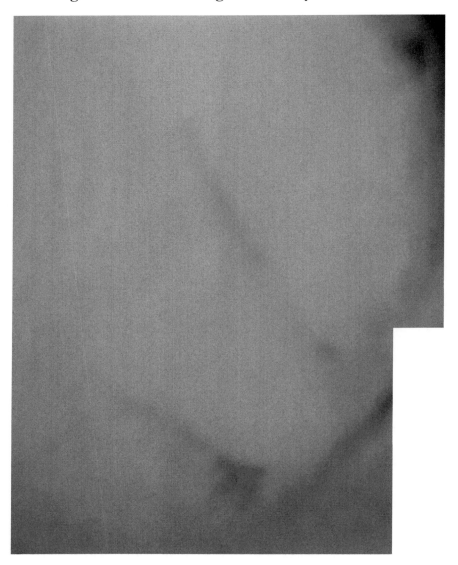

This is just one incident that I have witnessed. The image was taken a few days after, so the scars have slightly faded. With my mother telling me that she has only been slapped twice in her whole life, this image proves different. She decided to start lying so she could make the court believe that she didn't have any problems with her husband.

Chapter Five

I'm Still Smiling! :D

When a person has experienced something traumatic from the selfish reasons of another person or group of people, the survivor is always asked a question. "If you were to stand in front of the person or people who have hurt you, what would you say to them?"

I have had so many opportunities to stand in front of the people who have hurt me and it has always left me feeling very vulnerable because I never had the last word. I will finally have the last word!

A message to my father.

Did you really think I was joking when I promised you that I would tell my story and expose the truth? You tried so hard to keep me quiet yet you failed!

I didn't know what to do when I realised the truth and understood how much you had brainwashed me. Everything that you told me, it always involved lies and no matter how believable you made them, you exposed yourself in the end! I hope that you now realise how brave and how strong I really am because no way in hell was I going to back down from you!

I was only seven years of age when you told me that I wasn't good enough to be a brother in your family and by telling me how I could open the front door and leave if I wanted to where it wouldn't have bothered you, it just shows how much of a coward you have been from the beginning. You and your wife had a big smile and kept on laughing once I was sat on the stairs crying my eyes out. Guess what? Both of you will cry from now even though you may not show it.

You have always emotionally and verbally abused me since my childhood and you have even physically beaten me on various occasions where you didn't care about what you did and how. By supporting your eldest son and helping him get off sexual abuse charges, you became a perpetrator yourself!

The way that you controlled me, you were successful in keeping me quiet for a long time that's for sure because I was always afraid of you. What you couldn't control was my soul because when you push an innocent person who has done nothing wrong to you to the point where they don't care anymore, that person becomes the most fearless human being!

The fact is, you haven't just supported sexual abuse; you have also committed the crime yourself. A few years ago, you came home and told me how you were on the bus and while walking up the stairs behind a lady, the bus driver pressed down the brakes a little too hard which made the lady fall back onto you with no fault of her own. You then told me how this angered you, so you wrapped your arms around her and squeezed her breasts.

It shocked me and I couldn't believe what I had heard! You went silent and walked into the other room when I asked you to tell me everything again, so I could make sure that I had heard it all correctly. The reason why you kept your mouth shut and went into the other room is because you didn't want to hear the following words. "It wasn't her fault yet you sexually assaulted her?"

There is another incident which you told me about and even though I can't remember her age, I know that she was under the age of consent and it happened many years ago. Your niece came to visit and was staying the night where you found her sitting on your lap while she was kissing your cheek "passionately." The way that you told me every detail, it made me question whether you were telling me the whole truth or not because you have told me many stories in the same tone of voice and after a few weeks, you have told me more about what had happened.

You then told me how you slapped her across the face after a few seconds of having her lips on your cheek to stop her. As I don't know the full story because I wasn't there to witness anything, the truth is a mystery. What I do know is you don't always tell the truth!

It seems like you have always had a criminal mind because you felt that it was okay to brainwash me as a child and then take me to the police station to file a false report just to make it look like you're the victim when you have always been the criminal.

I was unaware of what was happening and even though I knew that my life wasn't normal from various experiences such as being told to stay up at night to observe your car through the window; it took me a long time to realise how you are to blame for how long I have suffered.

You talk about how you have suffered for so long and end up blaming every single person around you except yourself. I never had a childhood or a teenage hood but you did! You never stopped going on about how much fun you had with your friends in India and what you used to get up to. Even though you never saw your father a lot as he was in the UK working to send money, you were still happy and you have expressed that on so many occasions!

Yes, you have told me how you experienced poverty and also being kidnapped as a child to be used a drug runner, however; you didn't miss out on your childhood or teenage hood in the way I did.

This proves how heartless you are because rather than allowing me to be happy, you thought that you could write my future for me just so you could achieve your own selfish agenda! You should have been so grateful to have a loyal son like me because I never put myself first and you know that. This is why you assumed that you could use me, didn't you?

I offered to help you pay the bills when I was getting education maintenance allowance yet you took advantage which led me to almost taking my life because you never stopped emotionally abusing me and everything that you did; it allowed you to control me. I was going to leave in 2010 and once you realised how serious I was about it, your control over my life escalated to a whole new level.

My life became a living hell each day and any genuine parent would get help for their son or daughter who would be begging to be saved by speaking to someone such as a psychiatrist. This wasn't the same for me because as soon as you realised how helpless I was, you put so much fear into my head about everything that you could think of which made me go completely silent.

As soon as I started changing my life for the better, you became even more controlling because instead of staying at home how you had kept me; I gained my strength back which scared you. You became so afraid of me leaving as you felt that your plan wouldn't have worked otherwise.

You didn't want me to leave because you had one main agenda which you never told me about and you tried everything that you could to make sure that I didn't break out from your control. The responsibility which you wanted to give to me was something that I wasn't aware of until you showed me the envelopes.

The time when your wife told me why you both wanted me to stay at home, it allowed me to confirm your plan. This was the only reason why you took my life away from me and you didn't care about what you were putting me through because all that mattered to you was what you wanted!

Even when I told you not to speak about my past to me, you didn't listen because you wanted to make sure that I remained in your control as you knew that I would have known the truth otherwise. Guess what? I broke out from your control and it feels amazing to be in control of my own life and one that you will never be a part of!

Once 2016 began, I felt something which I had never felt before. Do you want to know what I felt? I felt ALIVE because in 2015; I told you that I would do something myself and then leave where you would never see my again if you didn't keep your promise.

I kept my word and you know that! Until I realised the truth, my plan was to hurt the people who you made me believe were responsible. After I realised that you were to blame, I wasn't going to stop until I knew why and look at what I have achieved!

The abuse that you put me through during the time I lived in your house has made me view your house differently because it's not a place where I felt safe, it's a place where I felt frightened for so many years so in my eyes, your house is your torture chamber.

Before even knowing the truth, I knew that I would have to fight for my innocence because there is no such thing as an easy recovery journey. Once I had reported the abuse that your eldest son had put me through, you became the most evil person that I have ever met because you realised that your control over me was broken, so you had one main aim which was to either make me homeless or put me in prison. This was the only way you would have gotten away with what you did to me.

If I can go through abuse for so many years where I am still alive and still so sane, then do you really think that I can ever be destroyed? The answer is NO! The only thing which can stop me from living is death yet saying that, I won't die as I will just travel somewhere else if there is such a thing as after life.

If you thought that your lies about me to the police on the 24th June 2016 would keep me quiet just because you made me afraid of being homeless, then you were wrong! It took me two weeks to get my strength back and once I was standing up again, nothing was going to knock me down no matter what I may have had to face!

You have always known how to play the system and as the years went by; you got better at playing the game. What you need to understand is that there is no such thing as a perfect crime because a criminal will always leave something behind. You tried everything to stay one step ahead of me and you even used your wife to get information from me before she betrayed me. You both stalked me by knowing where I was going and what I was doing and you made sure that you knew every single detail!

I see your relationship with your wife in one simple way and it's how a pimp treats his/her whore. A pimp would tell his/her whore what to do without a question and the pimp would always benefit while the whore would just remain a whore.

I don't know why you always found it a good idea to harass me during my meal times? It was either before I ate, while I was eating or right after I had eaten when you would approach me or send my younger brother to harass me. Guess what? Once you know the truth is out and how there is nothing that you can do to get away with the truth, every single meal of yours until the day that you die will be ruined!

At the end of 2017 when you received a repossession order, you tried one last time to control me by telling me two different stories just to brainwash me and the reason was because you wanted to use me for money. You didn't care about my circumstances because you have never cared about me.

What you didn't realise is that even though "you thought you had control over me," I was in full control of my decisions. I didn't give you the money because you made me or I cared about you, no! It was because both of my younger brothers including myself weren't going to become homeless just because you didn't care about paying the bills as your focus was more on hurting people rather than caring about both of your younger children.

You haven't cared about me for so long and that's fine, but to not care about both of your younger children and whether they had a roof over their head or not, it makes you one of the worst parent in the world! You speak so highly of yourself and how you're such a great father. Really, a great father? I don't think so!

You say that you did so much for me when I couldn't eat as a child and how much you cared about my life because you were so afraid of losing me. How you have treated me since the age of seven says a lot about how much you have cared about me! Every time when I questioned you about your evil actions, you always told me the same story to divert the conversation so you wouldn't have to admit the truth.

The day when your wife became pregnant with me growing inside of her, you made a commitment to yourself that you would be a father! Buying me clothes, paying for my tuition and my driving lessons are a duty of a parent to help their child until they can provide for themselves. If you think that you had a choice, then think again because you didn't!

If you had never hurt me, then I would have been so grateful yet saying that, the way that you have treated me including the years which you took away from me, I am not grateful for anything because you have done more harm to me than good!

In fact, I have done more for you than you have ever done for me because if it wasn't for my generosity and loyalty, your mother wouldn't have had a funeral, your eldest son wouldn't have completed his university even though he failed. Both of your younger kids wouldn't have been able to keep smiling and you would have become homeless a long time ago!

Everything that you have done for me has just been a show because deep down, your true intentions were always evil! You didn't just use me when I had money; you have used me since my childhood!

Everything that you had planned for me such as taking care of both of your younger kids including the house and doing the brick wall is something that you found yourself doing, didn't you? You know what they say, "be careful what you wish for" and "what goes around, comes around."

During mid-2018, you started planning to sell the house without even having a school ready for your youngest son. Even though you knew this deep down, you still didn't care because it was all about you and your wife. Since the end of 2017, you tried to do everything that you could to get away with what you have both done.

Guess what? You can never get away with hurting an innocent person because no matter where you run, you will never be able to hide! I couldn't believe what my younger brother was telling me. He told me how you agreed to his idea where once the house was sold, he would stay in a hotel for four days a week for nine months because he wouldn't have been able to complete his sixth form otherwise.

Once I made him aware of why your plan wasn't going to work, you then formed another plan of selling the house quickly and renting two to three rooms out in the same area, so you all could stay somewhere that way until your youngest son had completed his GCSE's. Your reason was because you had no money and every penny that you were earning was all going towards the mortgage?

You have told me that you built two houses in India which are worth over three hundred thousand pounds each. You told me that you don't have a plan to go back to India and no one is even living in those houses, so if you needed money, then surely you could have sold them and that way you wouldn't have struggled financially?

The reason why you didn't want to do this is because you wanted me out of your house and as you knew that it wouldn't have worked by forcefully kicking me out as I would have taken you to court, you felt that selling your house would be the better option even though both of your younger kids would struggle?

The house wasn't even ready to be sold yet you had put it up for sale? Any normal person would make sure that their house is fully ready to be sold, but you're not a normal person are you because you think it's okay to destroy someone's life and then do everything that you can to get away with it? It just shows your desperation for not wanting to get caught!

You can take me out of your will because I want nothing from you and the money that you took from me, it will haunt you for the rest of your life and after!

A message to my mother.

I don't know whether to laugh at you or scream in your face? What wrong did I ever do to you? You thought that you could remain safe by betraying me and supporting your husband yet you put yourself in a position which you couldn't control.

Did you really think that just because your husband could throw me out of his house if I was to speak the truth, then you would get away with everything that you put me through? Since my childhood, I was always there for you and you even asked for my advice when I was so young on whether you should have left or stayed?

I spoke up for you in the times that I could and I comforted you when you were vulnerable. I made sure that you didn't face the humiliation of becoming homeless, not being able to give your mother-in-law a funeral and having no fireworks for both of your younger kids during festival times.

You had the time of your life until you betrayed me and the times when you only spoke nicely to me after betraying me was just so you could try to use me! I wasn't blinded by what was happening because I could see everything clearly!

I hope that you're pleased with your decision because instead of feeling free; you feel so trapped and I could see the guilt on your face because deep down, it's been killing you inside, hasn't it?

The son that was always there for you and never did any wrong to the family was abandoned by his evil parents who thought that their agenda was more important. I even had to beg you and your husband to not make me homeless even when I wasn't in the wrong! That's how vulnerable you made me feel for so many weeks!

How does it make you feel by knowing that the son you betrayed was the one who exposed you? I have never been weak and have never run away from my problems! I stood my ground and look at what I have achieved with no help from you or your husband!

It must hurt you so much that you haven't seen or heard from your eldest son for a few years now? The reason why he stopped speaking to you and your husband after the sexual abuse case is because he wanted nothing to do with you both. If you don't believe me, then go and ask the police! It's very interesting how you and your husband supported him and helped him to get away with what he did and then he wants nothing to do with you both?

The time you said, "It's your fault your younger brother lost weight and if he fails his GCSE's, it will be your fault." This was only a diversion story, wasn't it? The real reason why you betrayed me is because your husband told you to choose a side and as you felt safer with him which I can't understand why, you didn't want to own up to the truth. This is how evil you are where just to save yourself, you made me experience such pain which you will always regret!

You will live the rest of your life in so much pain until the day that you die and because of your selfish, evil intentions, you will never be a part of my life ever again!

A message to my eldest brother.

It's been a few years since I last spoke to you and I have to be honest, I didn't enjoy hearing your voice the times we spoke over the phone. After I realised that you had abused me because you wanted to, you became a stranger and weren't my brother anymore. You will never be my brother because real brothers never hurt each other!

I get it, your friend showed you porn when you were fourteen and it messed with your head so you abused me. I did a lot of thinking during my recovery journey and I don't blame you for abusing me because when you're that young and innocent; you don't always know what's right or wrong. Maybe you really are an abuser?

Do you want to know the truth? What you did to me, it wouldn't have been reported to the police if you didn't betray me further because I always loved you as a brother. I was the one who looked out for you when we were young where I cooked for you, cleaned up after you and even washed your clothes when everyone else were in India in 2008. I also felt your pain when our father was beating our mother because I witnessed it too. The times when he beat you, I felt your pain too because as you know; he beat me on the odd occasion also.

It's understandable that you were afraid of him. What I don't understand is why you would lie to me about the abuse case in 2010 while it was being investigated? Why would you go against my words when I told you that I wanted no lies? Was our father's words more important than me experiencing the abuse?

Before he told me the truth, I assumed that you never betrayed me yet I was wrong and while you were lying to me; you were benefiting with money from me at the same time which hurt me even more!

I even felt guilty when the chief of police came to visit you at your work where your colleagues stopped speaking to you once they had heard that I wanted to take my life because you were taking money from me. That's how much I cared about you even though you were in the wrong!

I guess your heart is just as cold as your parents hearts because you weren't really there for me. You decided to betray me and use me which will haunt you for the rest of your life because when you have hurt someone knowingly who hasn't ever done anything wrong to you, the guilt never leaves you even if you were to speak the truth!

If you thought that what you did to me would break me where I would end up giving up, then think again because the people who are responsible are the ones who break in the end. The innocent who live through so much pain are the ones who are able to find peace which allows them to live the rest of their life with so much happiness and that is something you will never experience!

If any of you three try to hurt me ever again, then I will take you to court! I will never refer to you as my father, my mother or my eldest brother ever again because you don't deserve to be given those titles by me and all three of you will always be dead to me!

All of you thought that just because you would stick together with the same story to get away with what you did to me, then you would get away with making your side of the story believable. What you three didn't realise is that the more of you there were, the more lies were being told by you!

It's not always about having people support you because when you tell so many lies, you end up getting lost in them and that's how the truth then comes to light instantly.

It feels amazing to know that **I HAVE WON** and there is nothing that any of you three can ever do about it because you have nothing to hide behind any longer! Finally, all three of you have now been fully **EXPOSED!** Goodbye you child abusing cowards!

Chapter Six

I Will Always Win!

My life was always uncertain and painful until twenty-seven years of age where I didn't understand what would happen from one day to the next. It felt like I wouldn't ever break away from my past until I decided to stand up and stay standing.

By knowing how much I have achieved even when I felt so broken and helpless, it leaves me to say, **"If I can achieve so many amazing things, then so can you!"**

I will now share everything that I have achieved from 2014 when my recovery journey began until the day I self-published this book.

2014:

- ❖ I started and completed the Prince's Trust Team Programme.
- ❖ I started and completed my voluntary role at The Victoria Climbié Foundation UK.
- ❖ I started my Counselling Skills Level Two course.
- ❖ I started my voluntary role as a Young Ambassador for The Prince's Trust.

2015:

- ❖ I completed my Counselling Skills Level Two course.
- ❖ I learnt how to travel alone on the public transport.
- ❖ I started my Life Coaching Diploma on my twenty-fourth birthday.
- ❖ I won the Young Ambassador of the Year Award for London and the South East in the regional finals.

2016:

- ❖ I reported the final sexual abuse case.
- ❖ I remained a finalist yet still a winner for the Young Ambassador of the Year Award in the national finals.
- ❖ I started eating in public without feeling self-conscious.
- ❖ I took part in a formal presentation for His Royal Highness, The Prince of Wales at Buckingham Palace to mark forty years of The Prince's Trust.
- ❖ I completed my Life Coaching Diploma.
- ❖ I started and completed my business planning.
- ❖ I launched my Life Coaching business on my twenty-fifth birthday.

2017:

- ❖ I achieved my commitment in finding the truth.
- ❖ I released my Life Coaching Model and coaching programme.

2018:

- ❖ I removed my middle name.
- ❖ I released my new coaching programme.
- ❖ I self-published this book.
- ❖ I let go of the past completely.
- ❖ I started living my very own new life.

ABOUT THE AUTHOR

Shikesh Sorathia is a self-employed Personal Life Coach from the United Kingdom who has one main vision. **Every unique individual will be empowered to live a happy life by giving their new beginning their very own meaning.**

Shikesh Sorathia's mission is **to give individuals an insight into who they really are which will enable them to make the necessary changes, in order for them to live the life that they truly desire to have.**

Shikesh Sorathia's coaching is designed to take you to the very beginning where the negativity within your whole life will be completely broken down, in order to build you back up to the person that you have always wanted to be. This will allow you to live the life that you have always desired to have!

With Shikesh Sorathia's authentic approach as your Personal Life Coach and with his own unique tools that he has created, you will experience your very own unique transformational change.

To find out more about Shikesh Sorathia, please visit his website:

https://www.shikeshsorathia.co.uk

You may also follow Shikesh Sorathia on social media:

Facebook: https://www.facebook.com/shikeshsorathia

Instagram: https://www.instagram.com/shikeshsorathia

Twitter: https://www.twitter.com/shikeshsorathia